Now What's He Talking About?

Fifty Unorthodox Commentaries
About the
Central Minnesota Scene

by Mark Thelen

Also by Mark Thelen: The Thielman Building

Copyright ©2004 Mark Thelen
ISBN: 0-9763271-5-5
All rights reserved.
First Edition, January 1, 2005
All articles Copyright St. Cloud Times, used by permission.
Printed in the United States

Published by MK Publishing, St Cloud, Minnesota

Cover Photo: Self Protrait
Cover Design and Layout by: Randy Tenvoorde and Brian Barrick

TABLE OF CONTENTS

TABLE OF CONTENTS

TABLE OF CONTENTS

FORWARD

Why do I bother writing a monthly newspaper column? Because I get to grumble, show off and be a smart-alec on a monthly basis.

How did I get such a swell assignment? By begging - and bragging to Times Editorial Page Editor, Randy Krebs that I would write "cogently, wittily, persuasively and sardonically about issues." I had little in my background upon which to base such a claim.

Is it fun writing a column in one's local paper? It has been for me; people approach me and say nice things. I like that a lot. Not once has anyone said a discouraging word. Thank you, neighbors.

The Times web-site chat is another matter. My first column was called "drivel", my second "boring, a bit braggy and smuggish". And so it has continued for over four years without pause with such as "(Thelen is) a complete whack job" and "unstable". Surprisingly, these comments amuse me, perhaps lending credibility to those last two comments.

Thank you, Ann, for making sure my pronouns agree; but mostly for saying, when it was needed, "No, please do not even try to get this one published; we want to continue living in this community; don't we?. You still have time; go write about something else."

CENTRAL MINNESOTA BENEFITS
FROM FLAT TERRAIN?

Central Minnesotans enjoy ... can I start over?

Central Minnesotans have (that's better) a wary lifestyle built on a duet of resistance! Resistance to change and resistance to fancy extras.

But we better watch out! We must maintain vigilance of those forces and people who would callously sap the essence from the timbers of our great and cautious culture.

And my words can be believed because I have had my deliverance from a life tainted by whimsy and frivolity.

It came the first time I wandered from Minnesota. I quickly found myself clinging to the side of a Glacier National Park mountain face with a 1,500-foot drop below me. I was about to die. I clearly remember looking at my right hand as it slowly lost its grip. The next thing I remember I was 5 feet lower, staring in amazement at a path. Down.

> **"I rollicked, able to jump and totter and skip."**

Shortly, I was back on flat ground. For the first time in my life I was aware of the beneficial comfort of flat earth. I rollicked, able to jump and totter and skip, with no fear of falling to my death.

Well, that repaired my thinking. I came back home to good old Central Minnesota, where I belong. From this plain plane I should never have strayed. (Nor should you.)

MARK THELEN

I determined that I would never again elevate myself, and I would stay with people who can appreciate a flattened existence. Yet I worry. Even good and cautious people don't often reflect deeply on how important this flatness metaphor is to our ethos.

When I am invited to people's homes for a meal, I hear them ask God to bless only the food and the bounty. Thanks is never tendered for that flatness, which is our special gift.

Nevertheless, I see evidence that most of my Centriminny neighbors are committed to the flatland lifestyle. Mountains? Who needs 'em. We are doing plenty fine without them. Plenty fine flat.

But there are some among us who have not had a "trip to the mountain." They want to do things and build things. Things that are nice to read about in magazines, but we don't need that stuff here. I am sure the more careful, cautious reader will agree. And let us ever remember and learn from our past mistakes.

For example, that transgression so visible — the Stearns County Courthouse. Excessive. So much about it is unnecessary. What were our grandparents thinking? Marble and murals and a gross dome — a yellow mountain majesty.

Example two is the Paramount Theater. It was finally ready to collapse from the weight of its detail and extravagance. All we had to do was — nothing. But no, suddenly busy bodies stepped forward to save it.

Oh, it's pretty, all right, but is that what we are all about as a city, as a people? Pretty? Seats with cushions and goldly decorated ceilings and walls.

CENTRAL MINNESOTA BENEFITS
FROM FLAT TERRAIN?

What must our children think? What an example we set.

And please let's not even start on Clemens Gardens. A complete waste because so many of our homes already have a small petunia patch. (Which reminds me — stop planting annuals. Perennials are just so much more sensible. Practical.)

Final example: What's the deal with the Mississippi River? What's the point other than aqua-cartage. Civic leaders, couldn't we culvert and cover it? Get the new land on the tax rolls? Instantly solve all bridge controversies? What genius thought up that river thing anyway? And what were the real motives?

But be on guard, right now, today, right here in our river cities, people are trying to accomplish large, lovely, fun things. All of which will represent (cringe) change.

Things not absolutely necessary. Shout out.

Obstruct.

> **"Try to stay home more."**

We need only the simple, the practical and the necessary. Remember, everything is fine the way things are. We have plenty to see and do what with picture shows and Christmas and the tellyvision. And try to stay home more. There's no need to go out so much.

Originally published on 9.29.2000

Copyright *St. Cloud Times*

ATTORNEYS IN HIGH PLACES

HAVE BETTER VIEWS

No attorney jokes coming from this columnist. I like attorneys, especially the ones in high places.

I admit I know only local lawyers, but, hey, what's not to like. They are intelligent, caring, frequently drive really nice cars, appropriately pay for lunch, are often in possession of a marketing budget, can get you out of a tight spot and — and this is the real point of my deathless essay — they allow you to look out their windows.

Let me start with the penultimate attribute above, extrication from tight spots: About 15 years ago on a Saturday, alone in my office, the phone rang. It was an employee of a large, erratic, scary client. She had lost sleep, because as she told me, "Yesterday I was fired and I don't know what to do. I have been agonizing whether or not to tell you that he has no intention of paying any of the money he owes you."

Spine tingling. This amount of money if not paid would sink me. What was I to do? I wanted to call my daddy; I called an attorney instead, same idea though.

We met and after I told her the whole story she said, "Who is this person?" I spoke his very well-known (hasn't lived here now for a long time) St. Cloud name and she said, "Ooooh."

A knowing oh. An a-ha! oh.

I said, "Why did you say oh that way?" She said because he has a history of entering contracts and then, through his own personal cluttering, making them almost impossible to fulfill. He ends up with most of what he needs, no outlay of money, and his deranged sense of integrity utterly intact.

I didn't know if I should feel any better, but then she said, "Here's what I want you to do. Call a meeting with him and then bzzz, bzzz and then bzzz bzzz and then ..."

Well, let me tell you that everything went just the way she said it would. I remember that at one critical moment a look came over his face that

> **"(Expletive), he's spoken to an attorney."**

said, "(Expletive), he's spoken to an attorney."

I got every penny. Whew. He was soon out of business and honestly, somebody told me they saw him selling pencils on a street corner in downtown Chicago.

Thank you, counselor.

But back to looking out law office windows. It is the law that if you die without a will, your estate will be doled out to people you despise, even Uncle Phineas, already a blustering kabillionaire, the richer because of your inattention. Rest in peace.

So get counsel, but choose carefully. Shop around. Hereabouts there are quite a few law firms that do estate work. (True, you could throw a brick through a storefront window and get some defense work or you could get a divorce. But I don't feel comfortable urging either one of those.) I will not recommend a firm; that would be inappropriate.

But include on your list of candidates a firm of stature — as in height or "in high places" — above our mean topography

ATTORNEYS IN HIGH PLACES
HAVE BETTER VIEWS

We have a few with offices on floors numbered six or more.
And they will let you look out the window for a while before
getting down to business.

Looking out of their windows, seeing one's own familiar back yard from
these admittedly non-stratospheric elevations is (now you just have to go
along with me on this, a little faith and trust will help) is reeeaaallllly
marvelous. Fascinating. It is. Trust me.

I've been to the top of the Space Needle, the Gateway Arch and the
Empire State Building. None exceed the impact of gazing from the top
of our few tallish buildings.

"Oooh, is that the hospital?" "That (Division Street overpass) looks just
like the place Kennedy got shot." "I bet I can count 30 water towers."

I have actually heard sophisticates gushing such inanities. And the only
way to experience it in our towns? Estate work.

Unless ... unless someone starts a restaurant up there. That is what this
town needs - a top of a building restaurant. Maybe even one that rotates.
Who wouldn't dine there? Who wouldn't take every visiting relative
there - every time? Right? Daytime. Night lights. It'll be a smash.
It's just a matter of time now. I can't wait.

Originally published on 10.27.2000

Copyright *St. Cloud Times*

Over the river in 1973, my young wife and I immigrated to St. Cloud from Minneapolis in a loaded van. She followed me in our rusty Falcon with potted plants and two cats, Neptune and Poseidon.

On a whim we would start a business, Tetrasonics Recording Studio.

Why a recording studio? It was hip and cool. It was not well thought-out. In our first year, total revenues were $19,000, direct expenses were $13,000. That left $6,000 to pay the rent ($7,200), the utilities ($1,200), the phone bill ($1,200), and a few other bills.

> **"Our salaries?**
> **Less than zero. "**

Our salaries? Less than zero. Without even a delusion to call a good omen, it was a cold first winter in this new land.

But did we quit? Heck no. We had a vision, a quest, a dynamic sense of destiny. A hunch that pointed clearly to the unadorned, unalloyed, hard-earned, pioneering red-blooded American success that was to be our future!

Actually, no, it was a two- year lease that kept us going.

One thing we did have was time. Forty hours every week with little to do. Time partially filled with visitors, particularly area musicians.

Musicians worked nights and loved to come "rap" with us about their "gigs" and how, indeed, they were going to "cut an album" or "do a demo tape." But not quite yet because "our drummer just quit" or our "guitar player is sick."

Listen and react

One day, a visitor and I were rapping when I interrupted our important dialogue with "Shhh, listen!" nodding toward the radio as if an important bulletin were coming across.

It was an ad. My visitor remarked, "You always do that, then you grumble about what a stupid commercial it is and how you'd do it differently. You'd use this kind of approach and that kind of music and blah, blah, blah. Has it ever occurred to you that I don't own a business and that maybe you should go out and tell the dealership or the department store? Huh? Don't you think maybe you should go out selling!"

Well, I rejected that idea — let me tell you.

Selling is not how I wanted to lead my life. Pests. Intruders. Boors. Not impoverished nobility such as I! But then another bunch of bills arrived and I was forced into it.

Fortunately, someone else pointed out that selling can be described as telling another person how you genuinely believe you can be of use to them. (Thank you, Al Leighton.)

My first sales call was to a car dealership. I earnestly told him how I thought I could help and why and, and, and, ... and he said, well, he said he'd think about it.

So much for that idea; I knew selling wouldn't work. As I started to pack up to leave, defeated, it just kind of came out, "... if we got started on it today, Tom, it would be ready to put on the radio when the new Dodges hit your showroom."

He said, "Well, OK. Let's." (Thank you-ou-ou, Mr. Brown.)

Just like that, 10 percent of my prior year's gross revenue! Boy, was I glad — and obviously the new world's greatest salesman.

I headed back to "the studio" to share my elation (i.e., brag) with Ann when it occurred to me to make another sales call. This guy bought, too! Twenty percent!!

A tiny gear in the universe had just lurched. Our gear! Your town and mine went on to have the highest jingle-per-capita ratio in the universe.

In just two blocks in downtown. Tetrasonics produced jingles for Fitzharris Athletic (thanks, Lee), Jack's Outlet (thanks, Kleinbaums), the Camera Shop (thanks, Harry). St Cloud Men's Wear (thanks, Hermansons), Bachman Jewelers (thanks, Ted), and Metzroths Clothing (thanks, Mike Zapf and Don Hinkemeier).

Unfortunately, there still wasn't much profit in it, but then one day in a meeting with Terry Schmid of what is now called Lumber One, Terry said, "I sure like my jingle; Do you think we ought to use that concept in the newspaper, and maybe on some billboards?"

I said, "Hey, good Idea — media mix."

He said, "Do you do that stuff?"

I said, "No, we're only audio."

He said, "I'll write you a check."

I said, "Oh, yeah, we do that stuff."

There, right there, that was how we moved (fell? slipped? tumbled?) into providing a full array of marketing services and gained what ever success we have. (Thanks, Terry.)

A new world

I hope this story has read not as one of vain glory, but as one of thanks — one person's typical Thansgiving that when added to your's and all others' makes this weekend what it is — thanks to all those who have helped.

In over a quarter century, there were many more. But I'm not sure "thanks" is quite the right word.

Years later I was chatting with Katie Sanders. She, along with her husband, Dale, had started Tri-County Directory. They had competed head-to-head with an established, national corporate giant in the field of yellow pages advertising, and were successful.

I admire them. I asked Katie if she is ever asked about how proud she must feel for having accomplished so much. She said oh sure, lots of times.

Then I asked her if "proud" was the word she would use to describe her feeling. Without hesitation she exclaimed, "No, not pride, amazement!"

Me, too.

Have an amazing holiday season, neighbors.

Originally published on 11.24.2000

Copyright *St. Cloud Times*

'Tis quite the season! A season of much, including much bad taste. In the spirit of the season, however, we not only forgive it, we encourage it. Heck, we exalt it.

It is a season when tinsel and similar junk — boxes of the stuff recovered from basement, attic and garage — are reverently placed on recently whacked-off-at-the-ankles young conifers propped up in proud spots in otherwise impeccable homes.

> **❝I didn't mean YOUR sweater.❞**

Then, and without shame, we invite fashionable people over and they gush, "Oh, how lovely!" And mean it, for Christ's sake. (Precision, not irreverence, intended.)

Multicolored outdoor lights? Where and when else can you get away with such intrusive overstatement and not fill council chambers with enraged citizens poised to protect their neighborhoods.

But you know something? While I'm blowing the whistle on this annual cultural phenomenon, I am also admitting to liking it. It's fun and I really appreciate your forgiving me my trespasses while I forgive you yours.

For example, I brazenly wear neckties festooned with elves, lapland deer and men made from snow with carrots for noses. Into board rooms for seemingly important meetings I go.

How do I get away with it? Look around the room; Tasteful school stripes? Understated polka dots or paisley maybe? Not at this time of the year. I own a half dozen of these. Actually, they are among the better investments I've made: they signal to a room full of strangers that I am a friendly fellow — an approachable good sport even.

These are image projections that don't come easily for me the other 11 months of the year.

Women's holiday sweaters? Way too many colors and too vivid for the rest of the year, but magically "perfect for holiday giving". Yeah, right, perfect for holiday irony.

And what about those swirly marbly unflattering things for men who might better have gotten a health club membership instead? What's that? You own one? You're wearing one as we read? And loving it? I'm sorry, I didn't mean YOUR sweater; yours is very nice. Slenderizing even.

And the music. Over and over for over 50 years. One example and my point is made: "The Twelve Days of Christmas." See if just reading the first phrase doesn't have a Pavlovian impact: "On the first day of Christmas, my true love gave to ..."

See? By the time the turtle doves are mentioned, you're thinking about simulating a nose bleed and making a hasty exit.

On a ve-er-ery serious note, I want all of you who actually own the battery-powered animated dancing Santas to go put them away. Perpetual motion gives me a headache. I'll wait ...

... They're gone? Good, ours is now a better community because yours is a healthier home.

Food? As if we in Central Minnesota are stumped how to infuse ever more lard and its modern day "lite" enabler/substitutes into our diets.

Actually, I don't want to talk about holiday eating just now because
I just ate four big cookies that were made to resemble a donkey,
a Scotch pine, a clown and the head of a bearded person.

Now, come on, really. Be honest. Is this good taste? No it isn't.
Glad you are starting to see things my way.

While I enjoy all this in a rather grumbly fashion, I do also worry we've
gone too far. So last Sunday after services I gravely asked Father
Circumlocution if we had lost our way with so much emphasis placed on
the material clutter that has come to dominate the season.

Well, he surprised me by chiding me, saying that I should lighten up.
He told me he finds comfort in the enlarged attendance and the swollen
collection plates.

He said that if it wasn't for all the material hoopla, for many people
Christmas might be no more than say, the feast of the Ascension.
Which he added was actually quite a big deal, but not much noted
outside church.

Then he added that my concerns were entirely valid and the end
was probably near. He smiled, looked past me and greeted the
next parishioner.

Just a week ago, though, I was reminded that it is a season not just
about odd clothes, food and decorating. At work we participate in the
Salvation Army's Adopt a Family program. All employees chip in, then
we go shopping with a list provided through the Salvation Army.

Usually the mother writes the note, listing what we might buy for her
children, then adds that we should get nothing for her because if her

children get presents, then she will be happy. We believe she means it, then ignore her request.

Dickens' moment

This year as we were sorting the presents, I remarked how our participation makes vivid that there are families living nearby who don't have the bounty that I — and I presumed my colleagues — had always been able to take for granted.

To my surprise, two of my associates — intelligent, competent, and now quite comfortably employed — told me that when they were youngsters, they were on welfare and their only material acquisitions at Christmas was via such charity!

I was surprised. I also was surprised that I was so surprised, and I welcomed the reminder that a person's circumstances do not equal that person's worth.

Should I have encountered these two people a decade earlier would I have fully detected their greatness? I fear not. It seems I get at least one such Dickensian jolt each holiday season.

I savor them — all the while wearing my ridiculous reindeer socks and turning my attention to eating yet another half-dozen white frosted pretzels.

'Tis the season. Quite the season.

Originally published on 12.22.2000

Copyright *St. Cloud Times*

Before I allow you to read today's column you must be able to say out loud, "I love tradition. I love old buildings. I love our downtown." Done? Read on, we are in sympathy.

Something funny happened to the core of St. Cloud in and around the 1950s. Not funny as in "ha-ha," but funny as in something got wrecked and it can never be fixed. Something happened TO downtown, and at the time it was thought that it was happening FOR downtown.

I am referring to the first floor (sometimes higher) facades that were slapped onto our many charming historic (circa 1900) buildings.

At the time, "slapped over" might not have expressed why it was done. The Depression and the war that followed were over, and people wanted to ignore the past and bring on a new era of lightness and new materials, ideas and modernness. Let's hurry into the future and let's forget about all those bad dreams. And let's get going with You Tope Ee Ahh.

One good example is a facade recently gone but not forgotten — an icy sheet of shiny blue from the top of the street level windows towering up without any interruption and extending monochromatically left to right.

One-thousand square feet of indigo vivaciousness serving no purpose other than as a platter for four giant white letters: O-S-C-O.

Homes alone

Across Division Street, from the Father of Waters to Lake George, something else happened; we had many mansions. Homes of style and design and bulk. But they tore them down.

Who's this they? They is we. It didn't happen over — or by dark-of—night; it happened in plain view. We acquiesced. We still have a few. Beauties.

But go to LaCrosse, Wis., a community of similar size and vintage. Block after block of them, not here and there. Entire neighborhoods - square miles of them! Go to Hutchinson and Litchfield. Much smaller towns than ours, but many more fine old homes.

> **"Let's get going with You Tope Ee Ahh. "**

And why did downtown get a new facade and the near South Side crunched? They were not valued sufficiently by the community. And you know what "the community" is, don't you? It is us.

But now, some people, a few, care and are trying to preserve what is intact and restore what remains.

A few people caring may be enough if only the rest will help or appreciate the quest enough to not thoughtlessly impede the efforts.

What was that?

"When one dog barks, 10,000 strain at the leash"

- Origin unknown, at least to me.

A man was standing next to me looking down (pun intended) upon historic St. Germain Street from my second-floor office.

We were disengaging from our commerce and his comment was somewhat idle, "Boy, there sure are a lot of empty buildings downtown."

> **❝Me in full fulmination. ❞**

(Now please understand that my willingness to spontaneously combust into lecture format is — in my view — one of my more endearing traits. I bubble with enthusiasm.
So much so that I talk over others' words and speak with considerable loudness. Well, here was just such an opportunity and the rant that ensued surprised both of us.)

"And how many empty buildings do you see from here," I attacked ... I mean, I bubbled. He counted, then admitted, "One", probably hoping his cell phone would ring and he could excuse himself. No such luck.

I then required him to enumerate the fully occupied buildings within sight. It went on from there. Me in full fulmination. He repeating under his breath, "The customer is always right, the customer is ..."

But you see, many of us lovers of downtown must listen to such statements. Here's another: "Yup, downtown is dying." And another, "There's no place to park downtown." (Could it be that there are no parking places because so many people are here for our downtown's lengthy funeral?)

What if I said, "Division Street (or some residential addition) is dying."

Some would respond, "Huh? What the heck are you talking about?"

"Well, drive down Division Street and count the empty or marginal properties (or 'for sale' signs)," I would say.

They wouldn't like that statement.

"Seeeeee," I would wish to say, "Hurts, don't it?"

Our older central city is yours, including you in Sartell, Sauk Rapids and Waite Park. And probably St. Joseph and Cold Spring because St. Cloud is now a metropolitan center. To deprecate it is to dull its considerable existing glory and the hope of greater restored glory.

And because it is your urban center, I want you to consider that it — more than anything — suggests your community's vitality and health. It is a matter of pride, and your help is welcome.

Your help is self-help.

Originally published on 1.26.2001

"If dogs have a heaven there's one thing for sure: Old Shep has a wonderful home."

- Elvis Presley

Have you ever met someone and thought, "He certainly is intelligent. I don't agree with any of his opinions, but he certainly seems smart."

No, you haven't. So I assume we agree then that there is an equation between agreeing with people and thinking they are intelligent.

Tightly associated, too, is not agreeing with people and not liking them.

So maybe one ought to keep one's mouth shut. And so we do.

I, however, have gotten into this column-writing situation so I have had to think about things so I can offer to you my opinion.

I have discovered that when I think, it works, that is, I have reached conclusions to some really thorny issues. Big questions answered! I have not only thought about what baffles us, but also why these things baffle us.

Thus, I have wrapped up some weighty matters in a manner that should satisfy both those who have spent their lives confused, wrong-headed, or without any interest in big issues, and those who have been right all along. (It is nice to confirm that one has been right because it allows one to say, "Seeeee, I told you so.")

> **"Maybe one ought to keep one's mouth shut. "**

Now, mind you, I haven't figured out everything. Not at all. For example, where to put the Sauk Rapids bridge. I understand it has been decided, but the decision may be wrong or imperfect. Or fine and dandy, I don't know.

What? It still isn't settled?

Another example: Should one eschew confusion and spell your kid's name the way God intended, "Cindy" or jump-start the kid's personality and spell it with some verve, "SinDee?"

I can't help you there. You're on your own — it's your kid.

Here are some of the topics I have resolved:

Gun control.

The existence of God.

Which is the correct religion? (Possibly no answer needed depending on prior issue.)

Was Jane Fonda wrong to be on that Hanoi balcony?

Are taxes too high?

Why Bud Grant never won the big one?

Why was there a ring road?

Prayer in public schools (and all that related stuff like nativity scenes at City Hall.)

That UFO stuff.

Should 9-year-old girls take figure skating lessons?

Abortion.

Abraham Lincoln. (Didn't know there even was an issue with Abe, did ya?)

Should you buy a lottery ticket?

All that liberal vs conservative malarkey.

These are among those that come to mind. Some have ancillary issues that also have been answered entirely by one grand sweep of my giant lobes.

Take, for instance, that God thing. Closely related is, "Is there life after death?" Tell me, just tell me that you are indifferent to that question.

Unlike that Bud Grant puzzler, at least with this one, when you die you will either know for sure or you won't know nothing. But not now, not with 100 percent certainty. Not while you're alive. And you want to know now.

Or do you?

Don't worry, I ain't telling and I'll tell you why I'm not. Because there are many among you who wouldn't like the truth and then — here's the point of this exercise — they wouldn't like me.

And I wish to get along. Everyone knows that. A real pleaser, me.

You see, few are open minded. Thoughtful. Truth seekers. Considerate of other people's opinions. Even when as thoroughly thought through as mine are. Oh, and yours, of course.

So I keep my mouth shut because I must get along. But I am not feeling sorry for myself.

You have to conform too. We all do. That's why when we get together, say for our weekly Good Fellows Do Good meetings, we talk about football and snowblowers. By all means we leave the larger issues unsolved. Unexamined. Untouched.

But if any of you would like to know the truth, I'll be on the courthouse steps at 2 a.m. on the 14th of next month passing out my monographs.

But not in this column. Not in a town this size.

I'm chicken. I have to earn a living here. And so do you. Shhhh.

> **"Spell your kid's name the way God intended."**

Well now, I've enjoyed our little chat and I thank you but I gotta go. WJON's Party Line is about to begin.

What? It's off the air? Bummer.

Originally published on 2.23.2001

Copyright *St. Cloud Times*

Sports nicknames must be polite

Let's start with the easiest one: Washington's NFL team name, not pejorative?

It is as — heck no, it's more — offensive than those once common references to our neighbors who trace their heritage to Poland, Ireland and Italy. It's as disgusting as another word that I have not heard out of civil tongue for 30 years regarding our beloved residents who were dragged out of Africa. For money.

It is, among other things, not polite to hurt someone else's feelings. That's it; it is not polite. So it is irrelevant whether one intends insult or intends honor, the impact is that it causes distress in others, and that is not polite.

And so what if you find a Native or Polish or African American or a person without sight or in a wheelchair who doesn't take offense? Somebody does and our mommys and daddys should have taught us better.

And they (I'm still being impolite to that DC team) have the nerve to sell logo jackets. Maybe that is the answer. We can buy stuff. Money. Money. Money. Maybe the people who work for the Washington Rudenesses have sold their souls.

Get rid of that name. Move on and make money off of a different logo. The Washington Cocker Spaniels is available, and people love those little cuties.

How about the Washington Monuments? Think of the manly logo you could generate with that. And when the accusations start flying, you

could act as innocent
and bewildered as those
besieged Hooters
Restaurant people when
they whimpered that it
was "all about owls."

> **"Just imagine the manly logo you could generate with that."**

Right.

How about the Washington Tombs of the Unknown Soldiers? Now why would you be offended by that? I mean it as a matter of respect, and you can't prove I don't. As a matter of fact, I think my cousin is the guy buried there, and I know he would have wanted a sports team named after him.

So you keep quiet.

Closer to home we have North Dakota University's nickname. What? It's the University of North Dakota? (See where bad manners can lead?)

Any number of people have come forward to say this nickname troubles them. Why should they even have to? Others say it shouldn't trouble them, and then go on with the most tortured logic to explain why. But I hear money is muddying this discussion, too.

So who's right? It isn't a debate. Good manners are not determined by votes.

Say we have some people over and we know a guest has had a situation. A situation? Well, maybe a family member recently committed suicide. Or has been diagnosed with something scary. Or had a DWI. Or is bald. Or overweight. Or is Jewish. Or Hispanic. Or anything else.

(Your columnist is or has been several of the above, so watch it.)

We would want nothing said or done that would cause discomfort.

Closer to home, we have the Sartell Sabres, a little Freudian, but an OK nickname even if the only justification seems to be alliteration. Let's keep the Sabres.

The Sauk Rapids/Rice Storm? Now we're cooking. It actually has something to do with the community. It also inspires foreboding and dread in opponents. It is little wonder that Storm teams are awe-inspiring. Who can hope to defeat a force of nature?

How long have they been the Storm? Already I'll bet there is a whole crop of students that barely knows what it used to be. Let's just spare them that little unpleasantness.

> **"Who can hope to defeat a force of nature?"**

Why did Sauk Rapids change its name? Was it because the townsfolk are sensitive and thoughtful? Some, I'm sure. Was it because a vocal minority raised such a fuss that the majority decided to "let the babies have it?" Sometimes that is what it takes. Was it Department of Education regulations offering no choice or lose funding? That, too.

It doesn't matter. What matters is Sauk Rapids-Rice doesn't have to deal with it anymore, offends no one and is now in possession of the area's best team name.

Is Melrose still the Dutchmen and are their girls' teams really the Lady

Dutchmen? What committee or computer popped out that one?

> **"Let the babies have it. "**

Which leaves just one very special case, Cathedral's Crusaders. Apparently the Catholic Church's Crusades were so misguided and created so much mayhem over so many years to so many people that just more than a year ago — and this was a significant and historic religious pronouncement — Pope John Paul II apologized.

The events were so awful that the fact they were so long ago and there are no survivors, so to speak, didn't obviate the need for public remorse.

What are we going to do? We have a local Catholic school that has long been — until now innocently — named after a shameful set of events.

The status quo cannot be maintained, can it?

Wouldn't keeping the name trivialize the words of the pontiff. What is the right thing to do? Not the practical thing. Not the easy thing. What is the right thing to do?

But truthfully, maybe there's no problem because I don't think anyone else will mention it.

Too polite. That's it, too polite.

I won't mention it again and it will probably just go away. Then it won't matter whether it is a big or little deal. Or right or wrong. Will it?

Originally published on 3.23.2001

Copyright *St. Cloud Times*

What seems like common sense also resembles government

A bunch of families buy up some farmland on the outskirts, put in a fine-and-dandy cul-de-sac, build houses for themselves and call it something peppy and pleasant, like Honeysuckle Lane.

Yah, Honeysuckle Lane. All those in favor, say Aye. Opposed? Same sign. Done. Honeysuckle Lane it is. Happens all the time right here in Cloudrapids Parktel.

Then one of the families goes out to price a snowblower and says, "Woah."

So he calls a meeting and says, "Hey, neighbors, the snowblower that I think will work for me is $1,199. If each of us buys one we would have to spend $11,990. But I notice they have a real dandy that would serve all our needs for $6,000. Way more than I could spend and it is more machine than I need, but if all of us chipped in ... Then we could pay one of our teen-agers $100 each snowfall and our needs would be met and we wouldn't have to lift a finger and we would be money ahead."

> **"Suddenly, the idea seems to stink."**

All those opposed? Same sign. Motion carries.

The neighbors also suggest that the teen-ager must read the manual and be monitored her first time out by an adult.

Then let's look at maybe doing the same thing with something else where the same principle applies.

Pretty smart, actually, a group of people works together to accomplish a goal that is better handled than individually. But then let's quit. Enough is enough.

Does this seem at all reasonable? Oh, good.

But I would like to point out that we have just created a government. And we have just created a tax. And that adult is like a government agency. Making the kid read the manual is a government regulation.

And did you notice three paragraphs back? That "something else" I snuck in? That was the growth of government often known as big government.

Suddenly, the idea seems to stink because, as everyone keeps hearing around Central Minny and South Carolina and maybe a few other places, the government is always stupid and taxes are always too high.

Government workers (our teen-ager is one) are lazy and never as efficient as we heroes in private enterprise. Government regulations are crap and insidious, a treacherous intrusion on our way of life. And of course, it's all a plot.

Or so one would gather listening to the popular chatter, which is comfortably stated in public with no fear of contradiction.

Here is an exchange, the "A" part is commonly heard, the "B" part is not:

A: "Any time the government gets involved, it is bound to get screwed up."

B: "Oh, I don't know, I'm generally quite impressed with government services. For instance, have you noticed how bright, clean and safe a modern factory is. I think it's because of government requirements. And I'm always amazed at how quickly the roads are plowed. Those people are great."

I bet you've never heard the last half of this one either:

A: "Dang taxes. Average guy can't afford to pay 'em."

B: "My wife and I both work and we don't have much trouble making ends meet. So I don't mind paying my taxes and I sure don't need any rebate. I hope they give my rebate to somebody more in need. We've been lucky.

Honeysuckle Lane has demonstrated that "the government is bad and taxes are too high" is no longer an absolute and can be challenged.

Such statements are flawed, simplistic and not thoughtful.

But let's say you remain angry about government and taxes because your self- esteem is putrid due to a rotten childhood. (Bet you want your columnist to shut up and move to another country if he don't like it. Well, at least he should shut up anyhow.)

But I do feel your pain so I have some substitute phrases that should have at least some of the visceral appeal of "government is stupid" and "taxes are too high," which you must never again utter because I trapped you with my "Honeysuckle Lane" idyll.

Here are your new phrases:

Some government programs are not valuable to society as a whole.

Some programs are better accomplished non-governmentally.

The burden of taxation is unfairly distributed.

There. Now you have perfectly acceptable, intelligent comments. They should appeal to you because they are also negative. Negative and acceptable.

> **"Government regulations are crap and insidious."**

You may wish to practice them and season them with expletives. You will grow to like them.

There's just one thing more. You really should add something to each of them. As follows, respectively:

Which programs and why.

Which programs and by what mechanism.

How to more fairly distribute the burden.

It is a chore, isn't it? Issues involving government and taxation are complicated and don't lend themselves to single-phrase analysis. At least not anymore.

God bless you and God bless Honeysuckle Lane.

Originally published on 4.27.2001

Copyright *St. Cloud Times*

Threesome finds unique perspective with teen sensation

A teen-age golfer has been grudgingly taken on by three men in their 30s looking to make a foursome.

His name is spelled "Jesus," but of course is pronounced "hey-soos." He has a mature, placid style that unnerves the men, but they attribute it to his looking a little bit like a young Lee Trevino.

He whupped 'em.

The game was for micro-waved hoagies. We now join them in the clubhouse, where the three non-divines are finishing a beer on an empty stomach.

The kid has gotten them off their post-game buddy-boy banter too. It starts with Pete.

Pete: I can't stay long. I'm not just busy with golfing on fine bent grass greens. I also have to get out on the boat, and then there's the outdoor barbecues and getting new outfits so that I look sharp and tan and prosperous.

Matt: I know where you're coming from. Muffin and I are going out to eat later. God, can you believe the waiting lines? I swear, you want to make beaucoups bucks in Central Minny, you get one of those franchise restaurants and plop it somewhere on the West Side.

Jay: Ahhh, lucky us and don't we deserve it! We went out for sports and worked and studied and got a job and didn't slough off and now we are pretty comfortable. And prosperous. Money left over in the checkbook at the end of the month.

Jesus: It's a good life, huh, men?

All three: Eat your sandwich, kid.

Then one of them adds "But hey, hot shot, what are you gonna do with your life. How you gonna make your mark?"

Jesus: Not so sure, but I think I'll finish my schooling, then visit the sick. Maybe give shelter to the homeless, feed some hungry people. Hand out alms if they're still making them.

Jay: You know, you're kind of a downer. First you break par, now you hit us with goody-goody. Besides, that's not a career, that's a *sermon*.

Pete: But you know, sometimes I do wonder how I can be content when others are really having a hard time of it?

Matt: I know what you mean. I just hope I don't get sick. Or suffer a head injury. Or have my spouse walk out. Or get whacked with a bout of depression. Or lose my job. I'm carrying a lot of debt — it wouldn't take much to ...

Jay: You guys are all getting morbid. Here's how I can be content: I am comfortable and prosperous because I am special. Wonderful. I have character and an intrinsic superiority. I am, after all, me. Aren't you, too? Come on now. People who haven't gotten to our level of comfort, have failed. They are flawed and weak, aren't they. They deserve it. Or, or, or maybe they aren't quite human. It's God's plan. Hey, quit looking at me like that, kid. What did I say, what did I say?

Pete: I understand feeling like that, harbored just below the level of thought, but once spoken, it's embarrassingly not true.

Matt: Sometimes at night I think about stuff like "love one another." Sometimes I wonder what all of it is all about. I know it is not about lawns, long drives off the tee and making the playoffs.

Sometimes I wonder.

Right now a campaign is beginning that will enable our Salvation Army to build a Center for Hope and Healing.

The center will provide:

An emergency shelter for those with no place to escape the elements.

Temporary housing for individuals and families in various stages of recovery.

An emergency and supplemental food shelf.

Counseling services for rehabilitation and making fresh starts.

A lunch program.

The Center has already gained the support of Central Minnesota individuals as well as churches, businesses, governmental and agency leaders and many other organizations.

The center is badly needed and will be a positive addition to the community.

You can help. Everyone needs hope and healing.

Originally published on 5.25.2001

Copyright *St. Cloud Times*

> **"I am, after all, me.
> Aren't you, too?"**

> **"What did I say,
> what did I say?"**

"There's only one thing worse than not getting what you most desire . . ."
                                                    – *Oscar Wilde*

"We are not asking you non-Christians, atheists and Muslims to pray
with us...but ..for once let the majority rule instead..."

                                        – *Lucille, Times letter writer*

Kind readers, it is with some trepidation that your author offers his topic,
for it can elicit reactions that make road rage seem a meditation.

But if you take care with his reasoning, you may detect earnestness
and, he prays quietly to himself, room to agree. Trust that he is on your
side, though he seems an instrument of the devil.

You see, our topic is prayer in public schools and similar mischief
such as city hall crib scenes, mayoral prayer breakfasts and courtroom
displays of printed religious principles.

See now, devout reader, one sentence and you are already faltering in
you enthusiasm for this epistle. Bear with your correspondent.

Today's thesis: The more devout one is in one's theological beliefs the
more one should shun any association between public institutions and
religion. Those who advocate mingling theology and government,
should they ever succeed, will come to regret it.

What if our next mayor is a some thing you, me or we are not? And our
next Attorney General?

Have there been any moments when your author desired prayer in
public schools?

Desired? Yes. Thought it a good idea? No.

He comes closest, however, when he's feeling religiously wishy washy.

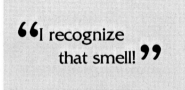

Prayer breakfasts with the name of a public office attached? Only when his faith is wavering. When he is feverish with theological certainty and frisky with righteousness, it is then that he resists mightily all generalized, indefinite, interfaith, multifaith, omnifaith, hedge-all-beliefs, nondenominational, ecumenical, nonsectarian, middle of the road, milque toast, one-size-fits-all prayers that must accompany such events.

Unclean, he sayeth. Unclean.

Unless. Unless, he sayeth, you beatify this unworthy writer by bestowing onto him the title, Tri-County Liturgy Laureate!
(Should we call him Larry?)

But be forewarned, what Mr. Laureate says, goes. Which, if you think about it, will be fine because Larry knows what's what — theologically speaking — for he was raised in a faith of religious certainty.
Absolute certainty.

Without naming it, ours was the one, true and universal church. Other faiths may have possessed a few truths, but only because they borrowed some of ours or because they stumbled upon them.

We weren't allowed to, in any way, participate in the prayers or liturgy of other faiths. Fortunately, no one forced us.

So, I am right and you are wrong. I don't blame you for being bummed. Luckily for you, here in America, you get to retain your tainted thoughts.

It is even permissible to believe (your author chuckles here) that your are right and he is wrong! But let us imagine, my kindly neighbors and fellow Americans, that we actually pass a law that allows and sanctions public religious expression.

Think about the consequences.

Who is going to draft the prayer? How will it be approved? Will it be so vague as to not violate anyone's beliefs? Or a simple majority?

And how is such approval measured? By a telephone poll? Put it on the ballot? Do we make it a Christian prayer? Or a "God of Abraham" thing to avoid Muslim and Jewish objections?

> **"I'm getting confused and my brain is starting to hurt."**

And even some Christians don't think much of saints, and that leaves out Santa Claus because he is based on Saint Nicholas.

You don't think so? I recognize that smell! It's the a whiff of situational ethics and didactic humanism, and it is coming from your direction! Ouch.

I'm getting confused and my brain is starting to hurt and it is warping my sweet disposition.

Why don't we just start to write a prayer?

Then let's just start praying and anyone who objects — why they are what is wrong with this country anyway.

Here goes: "Heavenly Father ...

What!?! You in the back row, you have a problem after two words?"

"Yes, I do. Only the third person of the Trinity, born of the virgin, took on flesh, so any reference to gender is tautologi..."

"Hold it, I'm Christian but I have a problem with that virgin birth thing."

"OK, we'll gloss over that."

"Gloss, Schloss, it is essential to my whole ..."

"What about the holiest of them all, Beowolf!"

"I'm Norwegian, ever heard of Thor?"

"Beowolf?"

Originally published on 6.22.2001

Copyright *St. Cloud Times*

Encounter with man raises some interesting ideas about freedom

"Nation wrestles with flag-desecration issue," warned the July 5 St. Cloud Times headline from a downtown vending machine.

I went on red-alert testing the wind for whiffs of flags in combustion. Suddenly, a man smelling of burnt silk, leapt out and grabbed me.

Let me tell you, I was frightened, not just for myself but for our republic. I was wrong, he wasn't going to kill me, he just wanted to sell me some flags. American flags. He said I should stock up because soon it would be illegal to desecrate them.

Well, that didn't make sense to me but, remember, I was shaken.

He explained that flags were now abundant because burning them was still legal and therefore, a hollow gesture.

Why bother. Soon, he warned, such banner burning would be illegal making it a sure step to one's allotted 15 minutes of fame — arrest, conviction and, here I quote the crazed man exactly, "if the abomination was desecration via conflagration with premeditation (flag burning in the first degree), the death penalty."

Weird.

I have to admit he had a point. Prior to this event, one of my few hesitations on the flag-burning amendment, which recently passed the House, was my awe that without it, America's freedoms confidently extended even to include the besmirching of this foremost symbol.

But back to my attacker, as he further demonstrated his constitutionally guaranteed freedom to yell.

He exclaimed — a crowd was gathering — "Where does desecration start and stop? We all agree about burning the flag. But what about flopping it around in the mud? Are we going to stand by while that takes place? What about using it as a tablecloth at a picnic? Sickening, but I bet the whole family gets off.

> **"What about flopping it around in the mud?"**

"How about patching your jeans with the flag? Six months in jail? How about a line of Old Glory underwear? How about burning a flag with 15 stripes and 50 green stars? Overnight in a minimum prison facility?

"What about burning a picture of the flag? Or a picture of the flag printed on cloth? I say throw away the keys. They'll say it isn't really a flag."

"Here's something else to boil your blood," he said. "People draping the flag from their windows and then (I doubt this will get past my editor and I am sorry for shocking you) leaning on it as they look down and cheer a parade of returning soldiers. It's right in the Code of Flag Display and Use. You have one in your wallet, don't you? Well, don't you?

"What American doesn't?" I stammered.

He wasn't finished. "If we finally do put a stop to all this flag burning and desecration wrestling, you know what those cowards will do then, don't you? They will burn some other symbol of this great land, like a copy of the Declaration of Independence.

"They will draw blackened teeth on pictures of our current and recent presidents, which summer time patriots might not think is too bad. After all, between the sitting 43rd and the recently retired 42nd just about everybody can find motive aplenty to reach for the felt tips.

"But let me remind you, some of these people are not desecrating the person but the office he holds, the office is a symbol of our great country."

"I say," he said, "Let us determine motive and throw them in Joliet along with the flag burners."

> **66How about a line of Old Glory underwear? 99**

He wasn't done and it was getting dark. Furtively, I had pressed 911 on my cell phone so the dispatcher could overhear.

"What about the flag of our great state of Minnesota? Don't you love what it stands for? How would you feel if someone burned that big blue beauty? What if the perpetrator was an outside desecrater from Iowa?

"What about other symbols of Minnesota; the pink lady slipper, gift shop reproductions of our State Capitol or an icon of our chief of state, Jesse Ventura? What if we caught some slime-ball stomping a bobble head of our present or future governor simultaneously stating, 'I hate Minnesota.'"

I heard sirens in the distance.

"I love Central Minnesota, too," he continued. "What if someone sullies a picture of the county commissioners? All such acts should make all true patriots fervid, screaming with tears of rage 'Protect us down to the last pebble upon which we stand.' "

The police arrived and put the man in prison. Loitering. Worked for me. Whew.

Originally published on 7.27.2001

Copyright *St. Cloud Times*

Now it's time for someone else to ask for help

"The land of runners-up" should have have been the motto on our state flag, not L'etoile du Nord.

The color of the state flag was and is blue; that part was correct. Until 1987, that is. Prior to that our habit of finishing second kept us frustrated and gloomy.

In 1987 our Twins became world champs.

Here's a partial list demonstrating our tendency to near greatness:

> **"Finishing second kept us frustrated and gloomy. "**

Super Bowl losers once.

A 1965 Twins World Series loss to Los Angeles' Drysdale-Koufax crew. Vice President (No. 2 to LBJ) Humphrey goes on to compete for the big one and finishes second to Nixon.

Super Bowl losers twice.

Vice President (Jimmy Carter's second fiddle) Mondale goes on to compete for the big one and finishes second to Reagan. Early 1960s Gopher football team polled as national champs but gets whupped in the Rose Bowl.

Super Bowl (that's three).

World Heavyweight Boxing Championship? An awesome power from nearby Bowlus lasts 27 seconds of the first round.

Super Bowl, yet again.

(Are you sure you want to go to the playoffs?)
Two Stanley Cup finals defeats.

Help me out, there were more.

But at least we are the Land of 10,000 Lakes! We're No. 1.

Yeah, right! Alaska has more than 100,000 lakes! Why don't they say so? Because to them it doesn't seem like a big deal; hardly worth mentioning. Geez, runners-up.

One day in 1986, however, without any deliberation or premeditation, as I was mulling my heritage of close-but-no-cigar, a discussion with God took place. I am not a religious person but I guess you could say I said a prayer. It just came out, kind of spontaneous like:

God, just once I want something Minnesotan to be Champion of the Nation and/or World," I said. "I want it clean. I want it unimpeachable."

God answered, "What about all those Minneapolis Lakers and Bernie Bierman championships?"

I shot back, "Before my time."

God said, "I'll think about it."

And here is where I blurted out a simple deal-maker of a phrase that changed the course of Minnesota cultural history. I said, "Just once and I'll be satisfied. I'll never ask again."

And I meant it. How many times does one need to be world champ? I don't want to be a perennial champ. Those poor hob nobbers in

New York (Yankees), those poor snobs in San Francisco (49ers) those poor slobs in Dallas (Cowboys.) Anything less than world champs and they are bummed out.

I decided that when I (you, too) became champs, it would be permanent. Well, you know that my prayer was answered with the 1987 wünderkinds, the Minnesota Twins.

And here is where I changed the course of history again; again through the practice of my simple, pure and innocent heart. I said, "Thank you, God."

God said, "You are welcome. Aaaannddd. ...?"

"And what?" I said.

"I suppose you would like to repeat as champions."

I said, "No, the deal was that we win big once and I would be satisfied. And I am."

And I was.

God said, "Wow, cool. I'm impressed. This doesn't happen often."

The discussion ended there and we've barely spoken since, but I have faith that because I honored the contract, God threw in a bonus, just as unexpected and inexplicable, the 1991 Twins triumph.

Deus ex Jack Morris.

I recount this series of events for you now because the Twins are in first place (I am filing this column two weeks before publication) and about to play four games against a team with the worst record in baseball.

MARK THELEN

Things are looking good and I don't want to have you do anything to goof things up. I wanted you to know the rest of the story so you could do what is right to bring about another Twins triumph.

But what is the right thing to do?

Pray for victory? It might put the mogus on the whole season.

Maybe God is waiting to hear from someone new. Someone with as simple a request as was mine. Someone for whom '87 and '91 are as ancient as George Mikan was for me. Someone with a pure heart that does not want Bacchanalia, just one sip of sweet wine.

> **❝I pledge to you, no more baseball prayers.❞**

For my part, I pledge to you no more baseball prayers.

I must maintain my ancient contract. So if the Twins are still ahead as you read this, you'll know neither I nor anyone else has spooked our storied 2001 road of glory.

I continue to think only of Viola, Kirby and Kent, then discreetly peek at the paper once a day to learn of Koskie, Ortiz and Milton.

"We're gonna whatever, Twins. We're gonna whatever ..."

Que sera, sera.

Originally published on 8.24.01

Copyright *St. Cloud Times*

Recently, I have read in the Times about people that I know; it's a small city. I have varied, mostly favorable, opinions about their talents and personalities. I know nothing villainous about any of them. And if you know them, my guess is neither do you.

But if all you know about them is what you read in our local paper, you think ill of them.

I am not saying the Times got the facts wrong or should not have used names or reported on these — and many similar — matters. I do say that the amount and position of the coverage, photographs, the choice of words, the size of the headline and other nonfacts create a sense to the story that is shrill or lurid.

At such times, our local paper gets me quite riled. How about you? Here are some examples:

> **"Our local paper gets me quite riled."**

Several years ago, a school district superintendent employed a consultant. She did her consulting and was paid according to the employment agreement. Then the school board became displeased with the superintendent and said so out loud and our local paper dutifully reported it.

Lots. Her name was featured in our local paper in a dozen articles in the course of eight months, culminating in this banner headline, "M--------- (I'm not using names) under fire."

She didn't do anything wrong. Nobody said she did. But a powerful impression was made.

Should she have been hired? Was she paid too much? Was she effective?

Think about most of your coworkers. Your bosses. Think about yourself. Same three questions always apply. Do the answers deserve front page character damage for several months? She got it. And was largely defenseless. I felt sympathy for her. And told her so. She told me, "Thank you."

The director of the local Y was dehired, released or let go. In our local paper I read the front page headline, "YMCA dismisses its director."

My understanding was that he took the job after the organization had found itself in rather desperate economic circumstances (from what I had earlier read in our local paper) and that there was considerable doubt that anyone could save it.

And he, apparently, didn't. And what is the quote from the director? "I wish the Y all the success in the world."

Classy for a guy in his hour of dismissal, wouldn't you say?

Now let's look at the recent St. Cloud school district levy scandal!

Geez, to read it, you would think we had our own Watergate or O.J. or Chandra had been found clerking at Crossroads.

Here's what we actually had: Many people who care about our kids' quality education quickly assembled into a group to gather donations and get the word out to our whole district about the need for an excess levy referendum.

That doesn't sound hard, does it? It is.

Then the levy passed and most went back to their jobs and to raising families. Then, out of hundreds of details, all but a few invoices get paid properly. Just a few, however, buried amid the thousands that the school district must process, get paid by the district.

And it may be a violation of a confusing and ambiguous law.

The total dollar amount of this scandal: $2,741. That's about the cost of one school district bus crinkling a fender.

Here is the Times headline, "Audit prompts criminal probe of school officials." Criminals. Lock your doors.

I offer this age-old tip: Don't believe everything you read in the paper. To be fair, any paper. Any medium. Even when the facts are right.

A school member apparently did. He read all about the levy, then felt compelled to fire off a letter to the editor that was oddly, both irascible and maudlin. It demanded a candidate's name be dropped from consideration as next school superintendent and that this person resign as acting superintendent.

And the Times not only printed it, they pointed the way with a front-page story. People were led to think unkind things about this human being candidate. People were misled.

Then the levy scandal went to sleep. Zzzzz.

It was roused, however, with a banner, seven-column-wide headline of a possible "criminal," of $200 donation by a well-known, local organization!

The reporting dutifully included now-sullied names of employees and board members who were in on the caper.

Mayhem of such magnitude comes out to $28.57 per column of headline.

Somewhat recently I saw a Times headline about a St. Cloud State University coach that was "dumped." Dumped? How about "let go" or "released." Human beings and neighbors are not "dumped."

I have little doubt that our local paper will continue all such reportage despite the impact on decent folk.

> **"You would think we had our own Watergate or O.J."**

My thinking is that they will justify it, even among themselves, using high-sounding and self-congratulatory journalistic policies and principles, slathering First Amendment unction upon themselves.

But I think it is the pressure to sell newspapers. Such pressure can mask that such harm doing to good neighbors, under any other circumstances, would make them ashamed.

It's a small town.

Originally published on 9.29.2001

Copyright *St. Cloud Times*

You like quizzes, sure you do. Especially photo quizzes. Especially this one - brilliantly balanced between ease and difficulty so the quiz taker feels the brain is still nimble and superior.

Your columnist feels he is smart because he made up the quiz and therefore knew all the answers! 100 percent. Quite a guy.

This photo quiz is about our downtown. Many of you like our downtown. Others, grumbly types, will never feel at home on any planet with even a single parking meter. For them, well, at least it's a quiz.

This one demonstrates that our downtown is surprising and interesting. I decided to do a downtown quiz after a conversation I had with some guy. He admitted that, though his 10- and 8-year old Burnsville tykes were already bored with Hawaii and Disney World, he had never taken them to their own downtown, Minneapolis.

That's neglect, if you ask me. The quiz will determine if you have gotten your family to our downtown often and recent enough.

Let's get started; sharpen those pencils and gather up the family.
This is going to be fun and no parental discretion needed.

What buildings are the following clocks, pillars and murals associated with? (Answers are on the page following .)

Later, get out the playing cards and show teach them Crazy Eight.
Family values. The times are so ripe.

Originally published on 10.26.2001

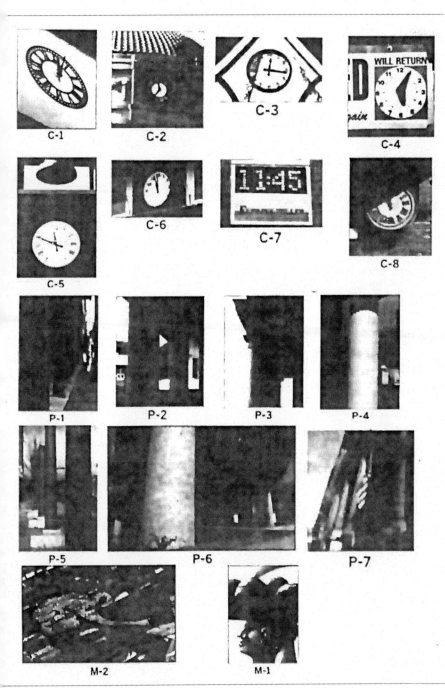

C-1
C-2
C-3
C-4
C-5
C-6
C-7
C-8
P-1
P-2
P-3
P-4
P-5
P-6
P-7
M-2
M-1

Answers to downtown landmarks

Clocks
C-1: Centre Square
C-2: Stearns County Courthouse
C-3: RD Miller's Auto
C-4: Lots of places
C-5: Liberty Savings
C-6: MTC Station
C-7: TCF
C-8: Pioneer Place

Pillars

P-1: Radio City Music Mall
P-2: Radisson Skywalk
P-3: Stearns County Courthouse
P-4: Quizno's
P-5: Courthouse Square
P-6: St. Cloud Public Library
P-7: Pioneer Place

Murals

M-1: Mexican Village
M-2: St. Cloud Floral

Ad intrusions have no limits

'Fake' ads permeate backstops, but are they really there?

Were you delighted with the drama and action of this year's baseball World Series? Well of course you were. Dumb question

But better than the baseball, I hope you noticed those advertising signs that were — as we looked in toward the hitter from center field via telephoto lens — on a low fence right behind home plate. But they weren't really on the fence!

Huh?

Yep, the ones where the message kept changing and the edges were always shimmering and garish.

> **"No listing in the yellow pages for "Ramparts.""**

I remember reading in a trade publication months before the Series began that such phantom advertising signs were on their way to our TV screens. It's the same technology that puts the first-down stripe on your screen in football.

That's right, there are no ads in the ballpark; nothing is visible to the live fans. The ads were on our screens though. We weren't watching the game scene exactly as it was, and they didn't tell us. We were being tricked. Hoodwinked

Lighten up, what's TV for anyhow?

Come to think of it, were those the real fans? They weren't? Cool.

Was that really Rudy Giuliani in Arizona? His presence had to be great for ratings. And why should New York have him all to itself? He's a national hero now. Morph him in.

But back to the signs. They were real, all right. Real fakery. You got to love it, and, of course, my opinion has nothing whatsoever, what-so-ev-er, to do with my ownership of an ad agency. How dare you — how dare you — even think it!

It was done, of course, in the name of advertising revenue. (A very fine thing.) But in addition to the issue of what is real and what is not in a live event, another issue emerges: Are there no limits to advertising intruding into our lives?

We hope not.

How far will the unscrupulous money-grabbing, mind-controlling, sociopathic advertising industry go?

I'll tell you how far they might and in the process make us all a little more whimsical and merry.

Benjamin Franklin — not much to look at but a real fun guy with the ladies in Paris I hear — had it right: "The price of liberty is nausea, constant hurling."

But let's have some fun right here in Cloudsarsauk Park. Let's start next year's River Bats games without a single "branding opportunity" unfulfilled.

"Ladies and gentlemen, please rise for our National Anthem."

"Oh, say can you see ... (You can't? Those visionaries at Granite City Eye Care can help.)

By the dawn's early light ... (Dim dawns need never be a downer again if you stop by Granite City Lighting.)

What so proudly we hailed ... (Crop insurance? Call Granite City Farm Services)

At the twilight's last gleaming ... (Granite City Car Wash can make your bucket of bolts shine again.)

Whose broad stripes and bright stars ... (Granite City Auto Detailing; it's your car, in a free country, do what you want with it.)

Through the perilous night ... (Public Service Announcements? Good idea: Our local police, protect and serve — day and night.)

O'er the ramparts we watched ... (No listing in the yellow pages for "Ramparts." Let's petition Congress to change the words: "O'er the strip mall we watched.")

Were so gallantly streaming ... (Gallant fountains, pools and ponds, too, at Granite City Landscaping.)

And the rockets red glare ... (Sunglasses from Granite City Eye Care)

The bombs bursting in air ... (Granite City Industrial Supply has ear plugs, safety glasses ...)

Gave proof through the night ... (Think she might be cheating? Granite City Detective Bureau)

That our flag was still there ... (Granite City Security Systems will protect all your valued possessions.)

Oh, say does that star spangled banner yet wave? ... (Permanents are

back and better than ever
at Granite City Styling)

> **"Permanents are back and better than ever."**

O'er the land of the free ...
(Perfect for promotional
giveaways)

And the home of the brave ... (Granite City Homes can build a home for
everyone including the very timid.)

Hey, this is the land of opportunity and — stop the music, maestro —
maybe this money could save the Twins for Minnesota.

How badly do we want it? Carl? Hellooo?

Originally published on 11.23.2001

Copyright *St. Cloud Times*

Hiring those closer to
home is smart

Firms can hire local people — and keep them from leaving. Hot dog, do I ever have a good idea! One that could make me a lot of money.

I want those area companies that assign their advertising budgets to ad agencies in distant large cities (almost always, Minneapolis) to award them, instead, to my company, Thelen Advertising.

Simple, huh? Dang, don't I love having my own newspaper column!

My idea will allow me to make buckets of money. Money, money, money.

Remember how the cartoon character Scrooge McDuck swam in his pool filled with the stuff?

Loved his money. I will, too; trust me.

One problem: I will have to hire additional people to help get the added work done. They would get most of the money that I should get.

Yes, jobs for our community. The mission of every civic organization, the mantra of every political aspirant. J-O-B-S.

Can you say tax-increment financing, land writedowns, below-market loans, credit enhancement, training subsidies, community videos and coffee mugs?

To illustrate, let us say that my firm's gross annual revenues are $5 million and I employ 15 people.

If it were so, that's three jobs per $1 million of revenue.

I know of seven local firms, whose marketing budgets are going else where and are large enough to equate to multiple jobs.

Of these, my firm could not do the marketing work for two of them — multi-product tie-ins, third world expertise that sort of stuff.

But the others? we could easily do their work — and in the process do some serious hiring.

These companies are headed by people who care about jobs for the community. They must think that great minds, real talent, is only to be found in big cities.

"Hot dog, do I ever have a good idea!"

Well, it is — and it isn't.

I have worked with people in firms in Minneapolis. Some are good, some aren't.

Hundred-thousand and million-dollar budgets really get serious attention at my store.

The good firms in big cities are only really stimulated from slumber by tens of millions.

Yikes!

Astute readers are already tracking that this isn't really about spending money at Thelen Advertising.

It is about local law firms.

Local accounting firms, local architectural firms as well.

HIRING THOSE CLOSER TO
HOME IS SMART

It could even be about other local marketing firms (but let's not get too carried away.)

Too simple? Will it work if the idea gets around?

Well, I ran the idea up a flagpole at a recent economic development meeting.

Mostly we all then ruminated, pondered and mulled the goal parameters, geographic modalities and inclusionary rubrics.

Nevertheless, it was a positive discussion.

Leaving the meeting, one of the participants caught up with me and said, "Call me. We're using a Twin Cities agency and come to think of it, maybe a local firm could handle it."

> **"Well, I ran the idea up a flagpole. "**

I did, and we are. And right there, one more job for our town was born.

Originally published on 12.28.2001
Copyright *St. Cloud Times*

Employees also should set realistic goals, keep a positive outlook

> "Every man is a piece of the continent ... If a clog be washed away by the sea, Europe is the less, as well as if a promontory were, as well as if the manor of a friend ... Never send to know for whom the bell tolls, it tolls for thee." — *John Donne*

Well, it is going to be quite the deal, isn't it — if a buyer for Fingerhut cannot be either formed or found? If one emerges successfully, this column is, blissfully, something in which to wrap fish.

Fingerhut's closing? This column will offer advice in that eventuality.

Secondly, I will give it to people who will be getting lots of it, the battalions of the soon-to-be unemployed. But first I wish to chat with those in a job-application-evaluation capacity. I mean employers, large and small, human resource people or anyone who just opens the company mail.

From now on, it is only common courtesy, as part of what should shape up as Central Minnesota's War on Joblessness, let anyone who contacts you seeking employment, by whatever medium, hear back from you.

Tell them the truth, give them some feedback and be nice.

Be nice. These people are hurting and scared. And it is painful and debilitating to try to make such contacts. And it is so much worse not ever to know if someone heard you. As if they didn't exist or matter. "Is anyone out there? Hello."

Companies these days do not respond with even minimal courtesy to resumes or drop-ins filling out applications. Drop-ins? Invite them in, ask them how it is going, get them a soda. Don't make them feel like low life. They aren't. Treat them like honored guests. Like friends and neighbors. Which they are.

Every resume should receive a reply. And a helpful one. Every phone call should be returned. Tell them you will hang on to their resume "just in case." Then do.

Tell them that if they just had a little more fill-in-the-blank training they would receive greater consideration.

And be nice. And keep your ears and eyes open so that you might tell them to "give so and so a call" and "go ahead, tell him/her I said to call."

I don't care how many applications you get, be

> **"I'm pretty darn good when I'm standing in front of people waving my arms and shouting."**

helpful and be nice. Looking for a job is one of the most troubling and scariest thing a person has to face. I know because I remember; I started my business because I was too afraid to look for a job. True.

Now to you people who are suddenly feeling very disrupted and scared, out of sorts, useless and hexed, that is, laid off or about to be; here's some advice:

You just got a new job. Does that seem like good news? It's in sales.

More bad news: You don't think much of the product you have to sell, and it leases for several thousand dollars a month! And you don't have a very positive attitude.

The product is you. Looking for a job is a sales job. That's right, you are the product and you are the salesperson.

But here is the good news. You only need to make one sale because you only need one job. And true, there are more applicants now

"Is anyone out there? Hello."

than jobs and more applicants than ever before. But you are the only one reading this column, so you are going to have a leg up.

Start each day with a goal. And the goal is not to get a job. The goal is to make four contacts (phone calls and/or interviews and/or applications filled) in a day. Soon, five days will have gone by and you will have made 20 contacts. Still no job, probably; but you will have accomplished your goal.

Soon a month has gone by and you will have had 80 or more contacts. And you will have a job. Maybe.

Now, change that number four up there to six and the next ones that follow become 30 and 125. But don't make the four into 100 because that isn't at all realistic. Take your time but use your time and keep at it even though you get discouraged. Pick up the phone. Reach that goal. The ultimate goal — getting out of sales — will just come about as by-product of the process of those daily goals.

And after every call, every interview ask yourself what went well and what didn't go so well — and how you can improve it.

Pretty soon you are very good at it.

Remember, your goal with the next contact is not to get a job, your goal is to make the contact and make it as well as you can. Be positive, be properly dressed. Tell anyone who might be answering your phone at home how to respond. Develop an effective answer to such absurd questions as "Why do you want to work for this company?" and "Where do you see yourself in five years?" Be as sharp as you can be. If you make three calls, no job.

Make 50, maybe no job. Make 200, a job for sure, probably. Likely, even in these circumstances.

I have quite a lot more to say on the subject. As a matter of fact, I gave a two-hour workship just yesterday at our local work force center titled "Marketing Yourself for that Next Good Job."

I've done seminars all over the country. I'm pretty darn good when I'm standing in front of people waving my arms and shouting. Normally I charge money but this is different. If any organization, any employer, any group thinks that I might be of help for a group of unemployed neighbors, let me know. If there's a budget, pay what it allows. If there isn't, I'll gladly do it for nothing.

I want to help. Don't you? These are special times; we all need to do what we can and we'll get through. And we will all be the better.

Originally published on 1.25.2002
Copyright *St. Cloud Times*

"Wow, better than the pictures." That's how I reacted upon experiencing the Eiffel Tower, the Grand Canyon, Hubert Humphrey and the St. Louis Gateway Arch.

"Star Wars," the Kennedy Compound in Hyannis Port, Mount Rushmore, the Golden Gate Bridge. My reaction to each of those? "Hmmph, yup that's it all right but it's kind of disappointing." Just one person's opinion.

One factor in creating a reaction is one's expectations — what was the hype. High expectations? Greater likelihood of disappointment. I was disappointed by the first movie to be a Time magazine cover story, the first "Star Wars." I thought it would blow my mind.

The first professional football game I attended was Super Bowl VIII. I was pumped. I was envied! As we entered Rice Stadium in Houston with our $15 tickets, I looked down at the players warming up. I was shocked.

People. Running on two legs throwing a football. What did I expect? I don't know. To this day, I don't know.

But aren't we Central Minnesotans all just "Barefoot Boys with Cheek" when we leave our confines and wander toward or across oceanic waters? Perhaps we are not supposed to wander so. Perhaps it is best to just stay here and examine what we have.

The list is short, though: St John's Abbey, "Cleminger" Gardens and Crossroads Shopping Center, but little else here is famous, so expectations shouldn't be a problem.

So, to create a list of great people, places and things in the area, I must discover items without benefit of brochures. I must do some thinking. Hmmm.

But why should I do all the work? If each of you think of one item — not that I want to limit you; I just don't want to burden you — and send it to me, then we shall have a dandy list, and I will share the huuuuuge list with you in a future column. (My e-mail is listed at the end of the column.)

Tell you what. I'll get you started so you get the idea. Here are four of my favorite surprising, unheralded Central Minnesota gems:

The water tower at the Municipal Athletic Complex parking lot. A water tower? Yes, but don't just drive by it. Pull into the lot, get out

"I expect nothing more than a wedge of cookie."

of your car and stand under it. Huge. A wonder. Take your kids. Visiting relatives will no longer wonder why you live here.

We live on flat land and great vistas thrive on height. So we are panorama-deprived, sweeping landscape-impoverished. Wait until dark, then go to the microwave tower north on 22nd Street South as you travel it west from Cooper Avenue. Wow! Because you have low expectations, this paltry altitude is enough to provide several ooos and ahhhhhs.

Zelda, the penultimate sampler lady at Byerly's weekly food try-outs. A transplant from one of the Dakotas, I expect nothing more than a wedge of cookie and little butter on some sourdough. What I get are weekly sardonic opinions on the state of almost any topic that comes up.

Maybe she ought to have her own call-in radio talk show. Solid opinions offered without guile.

First Presbyterian Church on the South Side. A classic, it appears large from its wonderful stony outside. But upon entering, you are cozily enfolded in authentic dark woodwork. You could just as well be in rural England. The building is the real thing, inside and out. Go to Fourth Avenue South and leave town.

> **"Nobody reads my column."**

See what I mean? So now, get your heads together and nominate places and people. A few guidelines are necessary. Don't nominate the likes of the Stearns History Museum or Whitney Senior Center. They're supposed to be great. The water tower is only supposed to elevate some water.

People who are bravely sick? The Times already does such a good job with them.

People who volunteer a lot? Nah, nominate them for the Mayor's High Five award. Oh yeah, this also isn't about your chubby aunt Connie who is really nice. Nice in Minnesota? We're all nice.

The people have to be kind of "out there," you know? This will be a tough category because, other than Mayor John Ellenbecker and Bobby Vee, we don't have many public people ala Connie Chung. Maybe we ought to just quit with Zelda.

Businesses? There must be something odd or terrific, like Central Appliance on Highway 10. It has a display of old-fashioned washing machines. I like it. Not suitable for teen agers.

Be alert, good readers, if in the next several columns you read nothing further on the subject you may conclude one of several possibilities:

The list above is comprehensive.

Nobody reads my column.

No readers offered suggestions due to the peculiarities of the shy Central Minnesota character.

Bunch of lazy procrastinators.

Evaluating the abundance of suggestions became such a tangled ordeal that I became disoriented and decided instead to write about the inequities of municipal water and sewer ordinances.

Originally published on 2.22.2002
Copyright *St. Cloud Times*

If you notice a few Delaware license plates downtown, it is because ING Direct bank is taking over the second floor above Herberger's and Ciatti's, and nine employees from the Wilmington, Del., ING operation have transferred to Central Minnesota.

Can't you just picture the family discussions?

"St. Cloud? Where the heck is that? Let's get out the map. ... How big a town is it? Look, it's right on the Mississippi River and not far from Minneapolis. What do you think, honey? Should we move? When should we tell the kids and will you do it?"

Wonder what they think about us now that they're here?

Brian Myers, ING executive vice president, (he's done well since his days at then-called First American) willingly arranged an interview with some of them.

You are going to like these people; they already like you.

The "focus group" never hinted at an attitude resembling criticism or condescension. None of these people faced losing their jobs in Delaware. They came because they thought it would be a good thing.

If you read anything here that suggests snobbery or superiority, chalk it up to flawed writing or self-esteem issues on your part. Here is what they observe.

They love Mills Fleet Farm because much of the merchandise (calf feeders, snowmobile jackets, tractor tires and big bags of gummy bears) is not seen there.

Crossroads Shopping Center is a "mini-mall."

They had no premonition that the first time they saw the Mississippi, it would be as a solid, that is, "totally ice."

One of them was puzzled one day that he was the only guy in the office. Why? "Opening day," he was told. This meant nothing.

Here people work from 8 a.m. until 5 p.m. Then they leave. There, people often work 10- and more hour days. But, they agreed, here people get about as much done because when at work, we work.

Here, everybody is always writing checks;

"Can I get you a pop?"

there, everybody uses debit cards. One went to lunch with seven people from Minnesota when he first got here. Seven checkbooks came out. Another bought a set of sheets and handed the clerk her debit card. The manager had to be called.

They were surprised at how the drive-up window bank people knew customers by name.

There, everything is open 24/7. Here, she went to a pizza place and saw a sign that said it opened at 4. That's 4 p.m.

There, traffic is always vigorous, rigorous; almost all stores are open. Always open. Here, her Saturn dealer is an hour and a half away. There, it's 10 minutes. Unless she takes it to a different one, then it's 12 minutes.

There are almost no status cars here. Like Lexus. There, he was embarrassed to arrive at work. Here, he hasn't changed cars.

Most of them were surprised when a teen-age boy started bagging their groceries at Coborn's in Sauk Rapids and Byerly's They rolled with that pretty well, but then saw the kid pick them up and start to walk out. "Hey, those are mine. I paid for them."

People drive real slow here; some even heed the speed limit. And we never pass on the shoulder. One person mentioned that at a four-way stop, everybody stops! Then three of them added, in chorus, "Real stops!"

One bought a house and was looking into a security system when she noticed none of her neighbors had one. She asked a neighbor and was told, "Nah." But everyone has in-ground lawn sprinkling systems.

There, there are many, many private schools, most without religious affiliation. And "everybody" sends their kids to private. Here, they learned that they might wish to consider public schools. No way — until they saw ours and met our teachers. And the school bus picks the kids up at the driveway!

We have three-car garages, "but you need them."

Yah, they say we say, "Bye now," "You betcha," "Say, I have a question..." and "Come here once." We say, "Can I get you a pop?"

"St. Cloud? Where the heck is that?"

Food: A few places here have something called Philly Cheese Steak on the menu. Trust them, it's not. They love our Great Harvest bread. One of them "would kill" for "real" sub sandwich bread.

We are less fashion conscious, more practical about clothes.

They like it here. One summed it up, "We gave up a lot of options but got a better pace of life."

I believe they meant it when they said we were "real nice and very trusting."

Gosh.

Originally published on 3.22.2002
Copyright *St. Cloud Times*

Noisy nuisance needs to go away

Some things are hard to keep distinct. Tell me which is the state that is skinnier on top, Vermont or New Hampshire? No one knows without a map.

Morgan Fairchild, Heather Thomas, Brittany Morgan and Heather Locklear? Who is which?

Bobby Vinton and Bobby Vee? Not a problem in Central Minnesota, but elsewhere it has been known to be.

And then there is Eurasian watermilfoil and personal watercraft. How can anyone be expected to tell them apart?

Both create havoc and chaos with the ecology of our lakes.

Both are transported from one of our cherished lakes to another by SUV owners who are either oblivious or indifferent to the damage they wreak.

Each hinders swimming, fishing and other traditional water recreation.

Both lower property values for lake shore homeowners.

Just in time for the summer recreation season I offer this summer guide with three ways to distinguish them:

Milfoil is a lovely shade of green, while PWCs are garishly multi-colored.

66Milfoil has no brain. 99

Milfoil is politely quiet, offering no noise to disturb your peace or that of sweet baby loons. Personal water craft make a loud, whiny, buzzing noise, without letup, for hour upon hour upon hour as it waves out at the speed of a bullet toward shore

"Flatulence is legal."

to irritate and infuriate mild and decent families only just recently released into the outdoors from winter's grip.

Milfoil has no brain. Personal watercraft owners do and most evidence to the contrary has not been well documented — although autopsy evidence does seem to convincingly show that that part of the brain normally assigned to social sensibilities is now little more than vestigial.

Because I hold with those that believe personal watercraft operators to have an intelligence similar to that of most humans, I hold hope that communication might be helpful. It might proceed as follows:

Dear Personal Watercraft Devoté:

You are probably nice, polite and not intending to cause others distress. So I am taking this opportunity to share my perspective, and that of the people who live in neighborhoods that have sprung up around Minnesota's valued, fragile, lakes.

I know that, once you have been made aware of the feelings of others, you will thank me for sharing and will be eager to cease causing additional discomfort.

Every moment that you are enjoying your youthful glee, those that live here must set aside their summer outdoor magic, go back into the house, close the windows, turn on the air conditioning and wait until you stop the @#$%^@# racket. (Sorry, got a little excited - won't happen again.)

So now that I've shared my feelings, I'm sure you couldn't possibly continue enjoying yourself knowing that so many others — too polite or shy to say so — are wretched because of you and your popular but annoyingly noisy machine.

Thank you for considering my point of view. I know you will find many other ways to enjoy your summer in a manner that allows us to enjoy ours.

—*Sincerely, Peace Seeker*

Dear Peace Snicker,

I saw your idiotic letter. I'm a water jetter and I say, get out of my face, you pathetic moron. Admit it, noodle limbs, deep down you wish you had the vim to be like me. Besides, I have a legal right to buzz our lakes and docks. And what evidence do you have that I am polite? None.

—*Buck Blaster*

Dear Buck,

Flatulence is legal, too. But we commit it with consideration toward folks with proximate noses, don't we?

—*Sincerely, Peace Seeker*

Dear Peace Sucker,

I worry that you have no zest for living as do lusty I. Perhaps if you just crawled in a hole - you'd find peace and quiet you crave. Above ground is really for us high-life, high-flyers.

—*Buck Blaster*

Dear Buck,

I can tell by subtle shifts in your tone that you are moving toward a maturity that recognizes that harmony among people requires that we occasionally stifle selfish "Wahoo" urges to move fast and drunken-like o'er roads, hills and lakes. Though I desire such thrills myself, I demure.

—*Sincerely, Peace Seeker*

Dear Friend,

But I spent a ton of money on the dang thing, what am I to do? Please help.

—*Love, Bucky*

Dear Buck,

I feel your pain. Those of us who have not thrown money away on such gadgets have lost money, too; it's called "the market." So think of this as your own little Enron write-off. Accept it; keep your machine in drydock and move on. Then maybe we can get together for an iced tea sometime soon. Gimme a hug.

—*Sincerely, Peace Seeker*

Originally published on 4.26.2002
Copyright *St. Cloud Times*

"I'm sure you couldn't possibly continue enjoying yourself."

This is addressed to today's young people.

When I was young, I received a fine public high school education and then went college for a nominal tuition. I refuse, however, to extend the same opportunity to you.

I have grown stingy and do not want to shell out the money. Nevertheless, I'm sorry and apologize. Perhaps others would like to join me and make it a class action apology.

Usually, an apology is accompanied by a statement of intention to amend one's ways, that is, to stop the offending activity. It can also stimulate restitution.

I don't see any of that happening here.

I admit to the irony of the situation. It is largely due to the educational opportunities I enjoyed that I could, if I would, now pay for your education. Yet, my spirit has grown mean and so you do not get the same fair deal.

> **"Having momsy and dadsy selling discount coupon books at work."**

I realize that my education was not free. My parents and their friends (your grandparents) paid for it. Some may argue that my friends and I should continue the cycle of knowledge and opportunity. But we are not going to.

Live with it. Get used to it. We've already elected enough anti-tax officials, and there is another election coming. You, kiddies, ain't seen nothing yet!

Live and learn

You will just have to deal with the fact that if you want an education you will have to settle for a reduced menu of courses and extracurricular programs.

At the college level, we want you to pay much more out of your own pockets.

High-schoolers, for now we are continuing to pay for some classes and textbooks, but not for unnecessary novelties like band, art classes, foreign languages and others not directly related to earning a living. Courses like bookkeeping are practical and can stay. You'll like bookkeeping.

Middle school? Selling chocolate bars and having momsy and dadsy selling discount coupon books at work will keep your educational experience reasonably rounded. It'll be good for you, too because time so spent will mean less time available for extra-curriculars.

So you see, it all works out.

The parents of my generation, it's true, overcame the Depression and won the big war, but then went under the spell of a tax-and-spend haze — it was like they were hypnotized. They wildly bought and paid for all sorts of extravagant educational extras, as well as other things such as the interstate highway system. They paid for it too. With taxes.

And that's the problem — taxes! Shamelessly building a better future for all of us, never fully realizing that they were losing their souls. Learn to say, "Faustian bargain."

Times change

But alas, the money's been spent, so we might as well use their stuff. You can too, go ahead. Compliments of your grandparents. Not me and my friends. We know better. We know that all that stuff costs money and the only way to raise the money is through taxes. And taxes, my children, are a no no.

(You want to know more about the moral decay and social quicksand of taxes and runaway government spending? I yearn for you to have it told far better than I — a simple keyboard-impaired son of a German grocer couple — could ever hope to. Learning opportunities are ubiquitous, ranging from several of my Times Writers Group colleagues to every minute of every hour on AM talk radio. This new thrift enlightenment is national. It's bigger than all of us and resistance is futile: be absorbed.)

> **"Get out there and sell those chocolates."**

Another reason our parents could spend and tax (euphemist tricksters might say: "Invest in public assets and build for the future" — but we're wise to their sorcery) was because they didn't have the expense burdens we do.

They lived in dinky older homes and drove pathetic 105-horsepower, manual transmission cars. Their sorry idea of a vacation was the Foshay Tower or the headwaters of the Mississippi.

We have little choice but to go skiing in Steamboat Springs for a week.

Our home must be new and 3,700 square feet with a three-car attached garage, entertainment centers and an underground sprinkler system.

Our "cars" are a van and an SUV and a pickup with a trailer to haul you and the four-wheelers up north. It goes on and on, these modern necessaries.

And don't forget, you live in that big house and drive one of those big vehicles, so you see how much better off you are? And happier too.

So get out there and sell those chocolates and don't forget to pledge your allegiance.

Originally published on 5.24.2002
Copyright *St. Cloud Times*

From baseball to religion, trust is diminishing

Who do you trust these days?

A Kansas City pharmacist, it seems, has watered down cancer drugs. Lots of them. A pharmacist!?!

Babe Ruth's 60 homers are surpassed annually. And by multiple players. Let's hear it for modern-day nutrition and improved training methods, they said. But now we are told that a lot of the required muscle is the result of steroids and that Major League Baseball does not prescribe their use.

Not so long ago the following sentence could be heard without cynicism, "Hey, don't worry about nuclear power plants, they monitor those things and have so much system redundancy, nothing bad could ever happen."

Here's another good one, "They (government/lawn services) couldn't/wouldn't put any chemical on our lawn if it weren't absolutely safe."

> **"I care about you, have family values, fly the flag and have plaques on my wall that attest to years of community service."**

Close to home

Recently on a television magazine show, a parishioner said she was concerned about the actions of Catholic priests, but she knew her pastor

could never do anything like that. She said, "I trust him ab-so-lute-ly."
Perhaps she shouldn't.

I have long flattered myself that I don't flatter myself with the following
statement: "I think I'm a pretty good judge of character and I believe that
so-and-so could (or could never) do such and such."

It's that "pretty good judge of character" stuff that I think is hazardous.

The "cabin priest," the one whom they also are wondering about
regarding the 1974 murders of the Reker sisters, was my logic professor
at St John's. (He gave me an "A"; trust me.) He was also my "prefect,"
meaning he was the faculty member who lived on "Third Tommy" my
junior year.

The former abbot who is accused of ... what? — I've become lost in
the forest of local and national accusations — was the chaplain in the
nursing home in which my mother was trusting her last days with the
Catholic promise of eternal peace.

Both men — in my experience — were pious, intelligent and kind, that
is, trustworthy. Which is not to say that I don't believe some or all of the
charges and insinuations are true.

Of bulls and bears

For a little more than a decade, like you probably, I have been "in the
market." I've gotten advice in the usual ways, including from some local
brokers. When everybody was making a ton, we were all geniuses.
When things went down — and down and down — we became timid.
Even paralyzed because "it can't go lower, can it?"

Down and down and down. One morning one of them called, "Yeah, you know Enron has declared bankruptcy and ah, you have a little bit of a position in it."

I said, "I heard it on the radio this morning," as I thought, "I doubt that's what they mean by inside information." He had, I think, trusted too much in the advice of his trusted research firm, Goldman Sachs.

Can you tell the difference between Goldman Sachs and the hundred million dollar finee, Merrill Lynch, who was "Bullish on America"? Or any of the other reputable ratings services?

(By the way, while our household generously participated in the recent bad market, we also enjoyed the prior decade's richer harvest. So, we are OK and you can put that checkbook away. Thanks, anyhow.)

Speaking of Enron, when I was an intern accountant at Honeywell in Minneapolis, the real accountants would hush at the mention of Haskins and Sells, the external auditors!

Whatever mischief or mayhem we "internals" occasionally exhibited through laziness, chicanery or dullness, when it had something to do with anything that the external auditors were to "sign off on" then, my children, that would be that, and we would become scrupulous.

Once I could tell you to trust the external auditors but since the shredding machines-gone-berserk of Arthur Anderson, Enron's external auditors, I can't.

Who is left?

Pharmacists, clergymen, baseball heroes, financial advisors, ratings services, auditors. What is this all about? That trust is dead?

Or that the vast majority of people are good and that our struggle is to keep our perspective while bobbing on a sea of disappointing news?

Who do I trust? Danged if I know. And if I did, and told you, could you trust me? Yes, of course you could. Because I care about you, have family values, fly the flag and have plaques on my wall that attest to years of community service.

And next month's column is about a fish I caught. Unfortunately, it got away and you are just going to have to trust that it was huge. Possibly a world record.

Originally published on 6.28.2002
Copyright *St. Cloud Times*

My September column created far more favorable reaction than any other. In it I luridly chastened the Times for "shrill" and "lurid" reporting of local events and instructed the reporters, headline writers, photographers and editors to feel ashamed.

The feedback indicated that readers were glad that I said publicly what they had been thinking in isolation. This support happened because — I believe this applies — no one likes a bully.

Thereafter, I set about to clip new examples with the intention of making an annual column of the topic. Alas, the folder is empty.

Your self-appointed ombudsman is rendered impotent by a subsequent Times staff meeting — I'm fantasizing here — at which someone said, "Perhaps this gallant Times Writers Group member has a point. Let's all try to do better."

> **"You cannot even go bowling with dead people. "**

And then they did exactly that, and I must give credit where due: Times, you have done a better — perhaps even a good — job this past year. Keep it up.

But ...

OK, fun's over, back to work.

Times, what the heck are you doing adding a column called Dream Zone? This is another slip on the slide toward non-credibility for you and America's media.

In Dream Zone, Patty Ann from Richmond, Va., writes that she dreamed a giant frog was on her bed. The columnist duo (with "degrees in dream psychology," one a doctorate, groan) tells her the meaning of her dream and instructs her not to do something she was thinking of doing. The advice: "Stay put for the time being."

You and I know this is just for giggles, but some people out there believe this nonsense.

Scary because we don't know what it is that Patty has not "thought through enough." Going to college? Marrying the guy next week? Getting that lump checked out by a doctor?

Dreams never predict the future, and if they mean anything, nobody can make better than parlor-game guesses.

To elevate them to column status is to imbue them with credibility. Where does this credibility come from? The St. Cloud Times. It gives a bit of its finite supply away to dream quackery. Quack.

Exhibit B: The horoscope, published daily in a medium that wishes to be taken seriously. Quack. Astrology is venerably old, but nevertheless it is junk science.

Let us imagine, readers, that here a Times editor broke in to explain that horoscopes and dream analysis are part of our pop culture and are printed to amuse me. Then I would ask, from the top of a long, long list, why they don't then report pro wrestling alongside baseball and football.

Also, did you ever notice the little type that says "advertisement" on the border of some ads in the paper? When the design style of the ad might fool some that the ad is really an article or news story. The paper is protecting the reader against thinking the ad has journalistic authority. Why here?

I offer here an olive branch to the hand that feeds me. "Everybody is doing it." It's true, but it is also a defense worthy of only a grade schooler lobbying hard for his/her first piercing.

Other media

My beloved and believed public radio, not too long ago, aired a few programs on "real life ghost busters." Quack. There are no such things as ghosts.

"The Tiffany Network," CBS, tried to boost its audience with a show about communicating with dead people. Yes, a televised seance.

Folks, you cannot even go bowling with dead people, much less have a meaningful chat: They are dead. That's what it means to be dead. Otherwise, dead wouldn't be the problem it seems to be.

One of the Sioux City sages, Ann or Abigail, has recently been publishing examples of dead people leaving pennies lying around so that grieving relatives can find them and say, "Hey, a penny from Uncle Harry, how comforting."

It became an advice-to-the-lovelorn epidemic. How do people feel who have not found a penny? Uncle Harry couldn't even take a penny with him? What if you found a penny and couldn't for the life of you figure who sent it? Maybe it was Abe Lincoln? Quack.

Some people believe this stuff. And they get to vote. This actually explains a lot, doesn't it?

Here is the problem: What is the truth? We can't all be a witness to events. We can't all run double-blind, rigidly scientific experiments to verify claims. We need to sense which messengers (the news media) are likely telling the truth.

I know that astrology is goofy. And that we have not been visited by space ships.

But it took me awhile to learn that the Bermuda Triangle and crop circles were hoaxes. And recently I heard about a whole process of evolution that has taken place at the bottom of the ocean that derives its fundamental life source from geothermal heat vents in the ocean floor.

Can we believe it? Not if we don't believe the source.

So, the Times, Minnesota Public Radio, Oxman and Fred Colby, Midnight Star, Entertainment Nightly, The Economist: If you tell me about homeopathic medicine, aroma therapy, "the Virgin" appearing to an area cheerleading squad, the curative powers of magnets, adding the face of Ronald Reagan to Mount Rushmore, or threats of terrorism at Crossroads, make it clear whether it is nonsensical entertainment or accurate information.

Big difference.

Originally published on 7.26.2002
Copyright *St. Cloud Times*

We are all tempted by something - candidates included

> "The more he spoke of his own honor, the more carefully we
> counted the silverware." —*Ifore Goetz*

Lust. Greed. Passion. Desire. Most men are prey to such evil urgings.
More so - or so I read and hear — in Washington, Hollywood and
elsewhere. Women don't seem to be almost so inclined. Yet, most males
in Central Minnesota lead lives of virtue. How, in a sodden world?

I have wondered about it, looked deep inside and have come to a
conclusion. I here and now extend my recently acquired wisdom to and
for you: We needn't feel so pleased with ourselves and need to quit
kidding ourselves.

We also need to be on red alert as we enter the coming season of election
brochures and broadcast ads.

You're welcome.

I had — prior to my colossal thinkathon — thought we are good because
of a childhood exposure to a religious belief very popular in this area.
(Licentious denizens of other locales have, at best, a corrupted version of
this heritage.) Yeah, maybe.

Similarly, I had allowed that we are true because mom and dad were
stalwart and honorable. They were. And it rubbed off. Virtue via
imitation, perhaps?

Is our exquisite probity due to a belief in, fear or reluctance to risk an
eternity of flames? Virtue ... or else.

Are we thus estimable because we have been directed down a meandering path of socialization and arrived at our truly glorious destination of goodness? Anthropological lottery winners?

Were we born with our rectitude? Is it genetics and we had little choice in the matter? Why not? Some seem to have been born bad. Why not born good? "Good seeds?"

One or more of these could explain our excellence, and what they all have in common is they make us confidently satisfied that we are good men of honor. Strong and noble. It shows in our brows and our confident gazes. Stout hearted men. Chivalrous knights.

Elect us all to something, quick before our ascension.

Yes, it is possible that we resist temptation because of nobility of character — and I so wish it were so — but I have to confess, the source of my virtue has not been definitely established.

"Hey, baby. Wanna gofer a ride?"

For, you see, at the first sign of temptation, before I have a chance to draw on any truly sterling quality, I first encounter something or other far less praiseworthy to keep me righteous. Convince me that you are different.

Here are examples.

Temptation: Cheating on taxes.

Estimable reasons not to: We love this country (county, state, school district) and could not dream of not contributing a fair share to its maintenance and vigor.

The real (operative) reason that stops us dead in our tracks before we need to access the estimable reason: An instant and clear vision of being hauled off to jail. To prison for life because it only makes sense to cheat on taxes (or rob a bank, or activate a Ponzie scheme) if it will add millions to elevate our lifestyle to an enviable level. None of this chiseling for a few thousand bucks so we can take the kids to Disneyland. Hard time, baby.

Temptation: Cheating on our wives. (We're all adults here, I hope.)

Estimable reasons not to: We have been very lucky. We love the women (and men) who love us. None would want to defile that wonderful outcome? Go ahead, bring on the sirens; resistance will be easy because our hearts are pure as fresh snow and because a vow is sacred. Because our loves are true.

Operative reason: When we were young and strong we were not successful with "Hey,

> **"Getting real drunk and ya-hooing a lot."**

baby. Wanna gofer a ride?" and other such antics. Imagine the embarrassment now that we are chubbier, balder, less energetic and lack all knowledge of hot music and fashion.

Humiliation and failure, not sensual ecstasy, are just a clumsy pickup line away. Powerful stuff.

Temptation: Getting real drunk and ya-hooing a lot.

Estimable reason not to: A mature and wise respect for our bodies and for the sensitivity of others.

Operative reason: Really painful hangovers. Twenty-four hours of remorse.

You get the picture. Mention a vice and then think about what really motivates our avoidance of it.

It is possible that we are — to our cores — honorable. But we don't know it for sure. And so, it is always unseemly, to speak of one's own virtue.

Who would do such a thing, you ask! A majority of political candidates, that is who.

They will compete with each other, comparing their family values to those of others. They will intone their love for all that is already loved by all. They will trumpet their trustworthiness. They will proclaim their caring for us, America and Haven Township.

If you met some guy at a social gathering, and within two minutes he volunteered a résumé of his virtue and integrity, wouldn't you think it odd? Wouldn't you quickly excuse yourself with a statement of a sudden and urgent need for more punch?

Get ready for it. The season is upon us for self-expressions of virtue, delivered straight-faced.

Don't let them get away with it.

Originally published on 8.23.2002
Copyright *St. Cloud Times*

Disparaged people may never know motivation behind others' actions

> "Who would bear the whips and scorns of time, the oppressor's wrong, ... the pangs of dispriz'd love, the law's delay, ..."
>
> — *Hamlet's soliloquy*

What accusations leading to what denials of intolerance will this new school year at St. Cloud State University bring forth? And then how will we be able to sort out the truth?

The mere anticipation reminds me that being a guy has its advantages. Well, mostly being a white guy, straight and able-bodied with correctable vision, not too fat or old, and money in the bank. All that kind of stuff.

> **"Maybe the would-be client is an idiot."**

Not because it makes one better, but because it doesn't complicate, in a certain way, so much of social interaction.

As in many other businesses, ad agencies such as mine commonly must compete for new accounts. Some company or organization says to us, "Hey, you and several other firms, come up with some cool ideas about how you think we should do our marketing, and — if we like your presentation best — you win."

When my firm enters such contests, we win some, we lose some.

When we lose, I wonder why, oh, yes I do. But I don't have to wonder if the reason we didn't get the account was because I am not white.

No, I am spared that little conundrum because I am very white. Central Minnesota white. I know that I failed because my proposal was less wonderful than a competitor or because the evaluation process was flawed. Hey, maybe the would-be client is an idiot and we are better off not to have gotten the account.

Our failure allows some questions, but none that have to do with skin tone. And it is a comfort.

Times change

Forty years ago, things were different here in Central Minnesota.

Oh, we had our little defeats, all right. At high school sock hops, guys would ask a girl to dance. Then she'd say her feet hurt, which made sense. When off she danced with someone else, we swains were left to wonder if something was wrong with us. What could it be? Nonwhites hadn't yet arrived in Stearns County. Gay — what's that? Liberated women? Huh?

Today, issues of diversity are very much with us though, and it is a complication and stress inducer.

But for guys like me, it's somewhat more abstract than for everyone else. Yes, life is simpler — especially around these parts — when you're straight, white, able-bodied and male. All that stuff.

Recently, I was at a red light on Division Street. In listening to something soothing on my car CD, I didn't notice the light change. Behind me a Camaro pilot did notice and promptly engaged his light-change notification apparatus and favored finger gesture.

The reason for his outrage was clear. He considered me a pathetic dolt — an impediment to his destiny. It was not because I am gay. I am not (or not yet out of the closet). No, the fault was mine, not my membership in a group that inspires rage. I was again thus comforted.

Recently shopping at one of our big box retailers, I couldn't get any sales assistance even though several customers had who arrived after me. That made me peevish, but at least I knew the cause was not that my economic potency was in doubt because I am a woman. (See Times Writers Group Karen Cyson's August column.)

Nope, I know that this episode was due to this retailer's customer service flaws. It was their fault and had nothing to do with any categorization surrounding me.

> **"His under-active pituitary causes him to feel chilly a lot."**

Many customers of the Java Joint wear black clothing in the hot sun. Last week, I cheerfully offered one some good advice, "Light-colored clothing, especially natural fabrics, would make you feel more comfortable than that gothic stuff."

The intended beneficiary of this fine counsel responded with an invitation to "get out of my face" and his opinion that I was "some kind of (I didn't quite catch the adjective) moron."

Can you believe it?

I retreated confidently knowing that this young person rejected my helpful tip because of a true commitment to the underworld, or because his under-active pituitary causes him to feel chilly a lot.

But at least I didn't have to wonder if it was because of my Muslim clothing. I dress "very Herbergers."

Oh, not to know

It must be difficult when a member of a disparaged group is put down, defeated, rejected or ignored.

How can they ever know for sure the cause. Everyone's life is full of "the slings and arrows of outrageous fortune," but some people must necessarily have considerable doubt as to the causes.

... And I had written this entire column confident in my lucky immunity from such doubt.

Then a proofing friend said, "... a pretty good column, not one of your best, but don't you think the Camaro episode, the shopping trip and the Java Joint dialogue were all intensified because you are not young anymore?"

Shoot, and it's going to get worse, isn't it?

Originally published on 9.27.2002
Copyright *St. Cloud Times*

My February column mentioned a water tower, a spot to view the city, Zelda at Byerly's, First Presbyterian Church and a washing machine museum as among our cities' great unheralded attractions and assets.

I asked readers for additions and got some real beauts. I present them here with no unneeded fanfare. This collection tells us unstudied and unrehearsed a little about our life and times. Thanks, readers. Your contributions are your reward.

Businesses

"...The little-known morgue in the basement of St Cloud Sewing Center, 3603 Division St. W. Rivaling the catacombs of Rome, it contains the remains of thousands of trade-in sewing machines, neatly arranged in floor-to-ceiling shelves, nooks and tables covering every inch of space.

Seems this repository is an international source for obscure parts for sewing people everywhere."

"Val's.: The ultimate hamburger joint now that 'the Flat' is gone."

"Anton's: Quirky little restaurant in the middle of chain-blandness."

"Gopher Bargain Center."

"'Books Revisited' downtown."

Attractions

"... The bottom (that is, the support pillars) of the Bridge of Hope in Sauk Rapids. ... It is like a cathedral down there."

"The tree shadows at 4 p.m. on the side of Coborn's Superstore in Sauk Rapids on a sunny afternoon." (Perhaps it varies depending on the time of year. Remember, my column ran in February.)

"... The Tech (High) School yard near the flagpole. I like to sit on the grass and enjoy the view of the park and lake ... years ago the administration planned to cement the hill. Avis McGovern, my neighbor, and I pleaded with them to let it be grass. They did! ... Walk around the building (and) enjoy the artwork on the old building and the spacious well-kept grounds."

"Cooper Avenue and 17th Street in the evening (before sunset). Look east and see the sun highlighting the children's home and St Benedict's Center!"

" ...(Holdingford Elementary School's) 'Dream Catcher.' " (I'm not sure that this fits my column motif; but how does one resist the rapture of kindergarten teacher Linda Harren: "... created from ideas by the children

> **66**What's a "motif" to a kindergartner?**99**

... (New York) architectural firm ... super duper model ... funds raised by staff and community ... truly a sight to behold and a joy to play on! Bring a picnic lunch!"

Besides, what's a "motif" to a kindergartner?

"Boy's Camp dam on the north side of Whitney Park. Sadly, vandalism mars the site, but it's a serene spot in the middle of the city.

"Hester Park's WPA walkways and bridges. ... Kids have spent many a fun day playing 'Billy Goat's Gruff' there."

"The Sis Castle."

"Sandy, the mechanical horse at Coborn's Superstore. Best bargain in town at a penny a ride!"

"601 Third Ave. N, Sauk Rapids, where the whole yard is filled with stone formations ... built by Louie Manea years ago."

The Poor Clare's Monastery, where you pull a gong to talk to a nun and most of them are cloistered in that place for their entire existence."

" ... Huge antique urinal in the men's room at the Fifth Avenue Theater. ... (It) is called 'the King' and others of its kind have been removed over the years because babies were known to drown in them."

> **"I pleaded with them to let it be grass."**

" ... Along the lines (pun intended) of your water tower recommendation, go to the anchoring spots for the guy wires and the actual antennae behind and around Regent Broadcasting on Lincoln Avenue Southeast. Totally awesome, dude."

People

"Jim Gammel, wherever you find him."

"Gary Zimmerman, the local TV star and grocery bagger."

"Andy Virden, the out-going blind guy."

"Jerene Herzing, the zealous and explosively friendly post office window clerk who lives with 30 handicapped cats."

"Those two guys who do movie reviews on public access TV with the pinball machine ..."

"Bob Eschen, the very large guy who washes windows for a living."

"... Super Fan, who comes to all the Tech athletic events with ... a very loud voice."

"(That) very tall and very thin guy with very long hair who" (has been running a long time around town).

"There are all sorts of characters at the Java Joint." (My comment: They're trying too hard.)

"Duane Even, the guy who bikes around town with very upright posture, usually wearing ear flaps and brown clothes collecting aluminum cans."

"If it can be worked out, a coffee break with Larry Haws."

From the Web

"Wastewater treatment plant."

"The Reformatory's 'Anal-Found Contraband' museum."

"Val's (hamburger shop) on the East Side."

Sources

Thanks to these people: Sharon Voss, Marie McConnell, Pat and Jim Gruenke, Pat and Jim's kid, Jerry Benusa, Frank Miler, Carol Barthel, Gary Osberg, Linda Harren, Bobbi Lampi and anonymous. And under cover of Internet: D, Chet, Lefty, Ed, Patastic, Bum, Dorrie.

Originally published on 10.25.2002
Copyright *St. Cloud Times*

Editor's note: Columnist Mark Thelen is a member of the St. Cloud Area Chamber of Commerce political action committee. Today and Saturday, he details the PAC's endorsement process for this year's elections.

Sept. 23

I worried that the new political action committee established by the St. Cloud Area Chamber of Commerce last year would be nothing more than a rubber stamp for candidates and issues that I was — how should I put this — unfond of.

Would the members with opinions similar to mine be under-represented? I wondered how a person became a member of the PAC. Who did one have to know? How rich did one have to be? Did they only accept conservatives? Would thoughtful progressives such as me be politely excluded?

I was getting myself all steamed up. Why couldn't I be a member? After all, I have been paying Chamber dues for 30 years. So I thought I'd just stir things up a bit. I called Teresa Bohnen, the Chamber's executive director, and challenged her with a question, sinisterly hoping to disarm with its directness:

"Hi, Teresa; Mark here. Say, how does one get on that PAC of yours?"

Her response was, "Would you like to be on it?"

"Um, ah ... well ... sure."

"Great," she said. "The first meeting is next Friday at 7:30."

Just like that and I was in. Apparently, all any Chamber member had to do was ask, so long as they held a substantial management position within a Central Minnesota member organization.

I have now been a member for more than a year, making the current election season our second; we cut our teeth last fall on school board and city elections.

I recall showing up for the first meeting with a residue of feeling that I would be an antagonist. I would take positions contrary to those of the other members, then listen as my profound, knowledgeable, multi-layered opinions were greeted with polite-yet-derisive, bumper sticker rebukes.

Then they'd vote the question and I would find myself again on the losing end.

I was wrong.

While some of the members were of unknown political persuasion, others were reputed to be quite a distance thataway "from center." If true, I found it hard — merely based on the discussions as they took place — to get a good fix on their political ideologies.

The members demonstrated no rigidity and most issues were discussed inquisitively. Nary a cliche was heard.

Thus the course of the discussions shifted, seeming to head one way, then another, then back again or off in a surprising direction.

I started to look forward to these early morning meetings. They were — interesting!

> **"I would find myself again on the losing end."**

At least, that's how it had been last year and in the several meetings preparatory to this season's endorsement meetings.

Today we heard gubernatorial candidates debating at the Civic Center. I will enter tomorrow morning's discussion favoring one of the four and sharply opposed to another. A third seems out of the running and the fourth I could accept as a worthy compromise. How will the group see it?

Sept. 25

As PAC members, we can vote for a candidate however we want in November. But in these meetings, our discussion and vote should be confined to the PAC's mission: To endorse electable candidates good for business in Central Minnesota.

After well over an hour of discussion, we endorsed Tim Penny for governor.

Critical determinants were Roger Moe's explicit opposition to workers' compensation reform; Ken Pentel's low probability of being elected; and Tim Pawlenty's lack of support for transportation issues that have received the local Chamber's support — most notably the Northstar Corridor and a gas tax increase. Penny generally had high marks and took no missteps. The endorsement was unanimous.

Weeks 2 and 3

We sat down yesterday morning to review the information we had (including debates involving three races) for two state Senate races and one for the House. We endorsed Doug Stang and Dave Kleis, both incumbents. While there was never much doubt about these endorsements, there was agreement that both could do a better job than they had in the past and we will be watching.

The surprise was the endorsement of Democrat Lynn Schurman for Senate. She was running against incumbent Michelle Fischbach.

Schurman caught all of us by surprise in her debate performance, hitting the mark again and again, winning the endorsement.

Later ..

We are getting feedback. Most notably, it comes from a few Chamber members who are upset that we didn't vote the way they would have wished.

The most surprising call, though, came from the Minnesota Chamber of Commerce. An official there asked us to reconsider (change?) our vote on the governor's race and endorse Pawlenty.

We gave it no more than a moment's consideration. If we were to change our vote because of a phone call, would the Minnesota Chamber look good or be a bully? Would our local Chamber be lackeys? Would the PAC become a rubber stamp? Would it have been good publicity for Tim Pawlenty, a tool of big business?

No, a bad idea all around. And, I notice, we members take pride in our independence and our desire to maintain our integrity.

Coming Saturday: The PAC Diary concludes as feedback grows troublesome.

Originally published on 11.22.2002
Copyright *St. Cloud Times*

Editor's note: Columnist Mark Thelen is a member of the St. Cloud Area Chamber of Commerce political action committee. This concludes a two-part column on the PAC's endorsement process for this year's elections.

Week 3

Rep. Jim Knoblach captured our endorsement in the District 15A race with little trouble. I suspect it would not have been so easy had the Democrats run a more aggressive opponent.

But other discussion within the meeting centered on the possibility of revisiting the Lynn Schurman nomination. Her opponent, Republican Michelle Fischbach, is favored by a few vocal Chamber members. And they let us know it. More than one prominent (read huge-dues paying) Chamber member went vociferously beyond "Gee willikers, I had hoped you would have seen the value of my favored candidate. What a disappointment."

How do we handle this? Do we merely shrug it off and let the chips fall where they may? Some of these could be big chips.

Do we revisit our past vote and do what we think the members want? The discussion was — ummmm ... lively.

Subsequent to the meeting, things only got worse. We had idealistically dipped our naive toes in the warm soothing pool of American democracy to do our part for all that freedom represents. And we are getting nipped.

One of us found it necessary to resign. Apparently, the impact of that person's membership (and presumed voting record) has resulted in the suggestion that the organization for whom that person works will be substantially and negatively impacted.

I had heard that politics can be rough, but I thought not here in our warm-hearted little River City. Your bare-foot reporter and patriot is troubled.

Next Wednesday, we vote on a House race. Will I still have complete confidence that there will not be invisible forces at work to assure that the vote is free and open?

I don't know. Stay tuned.

Oct. 23

Endorsing Reps. Joe Opatz in District 15B and Leslie Schumacher in District 16B was direct and quick.

> **"Your bare-foot reporter and patriot is troubled."**

We spent more time arriving at our endorsement of Dan Severson House District 14A. We then briefly discussed heated feedback from supporters of non-endorsees.

Please note such negative feedback is heard only when a Republican failed to gain our endorsement. That is probably because only they would expect an endorsement from a political action committee created by a Chamber of Commerce.

The elapse of a week seems to have calmed the situation, and the members agree that a steadfast commitment to our mission is the only acceptable course. I wondered out loud, however, to what extent we were (perhaps subliminally) influenced in our latter endorsements.

I urged everyone to consider how each would be able to maintain calm if three disgruntled citizens, knowing of membership in the PAC, threatened to take their substantial business elsewhere.

We have now completed our endorsement process for this election season. Disagreements were aired, axes were ground but no hatchets need burying. Friendships were begun. The Chamber of Commerce set this mechanism in motion to identify, support and endorse candidates good for business in Central Minnesota. This — subject to human error — we did.

> **"Dang, thoughtfulness and earnestness can be such a burden."**

The challenge will be to maintain the group as fair and impartial.

After the election

The legislative results are in. Seemingly, we helped elect one senator and three representatives. On the other hand, we now have a governor, a senator and a representative who will, I fear, remember very well that they were not endorsed "up in St Cloud."

Will the community pay a price for our little exercise in civics? Is it worth it?

MARK THELEN

We demonstrated non-partisanship. But if ever there was a year in which we would have been better off endorsing all Republicans, this was it.

Dang, thoughtfulness and earnestness can be such a burden.

Originally published on 11.23.2002
Copyright *St. Cloud Times*

Information on old tenants will help preserve history

In the late afternoon, Christmas Eve, St Cloud's ablest and best-known attorney stopped off at the Elks Club (now Pioneer Place) on downtown's Fifth Avenue.

He was a very articulate man with a good sense of humor and had many brilliant successes in his career. He called home (328 Fourth Ave. S) about five in the afternoon to say he would be there in a few minutes.

A half-hour later, Dr. V. H. Ernst found John Sullivan's body near the entrance to Central Junior High (now St Cloud's city office building) a little more than a block away. He'd had a heart attack. He was 71.

His body was taken to the home of his son, Henry (309 Third Ave. S). He was 71.

That was 1933, and while the Sullivans no longer live at either residence, both homes are still quite grand.

In an article about his death the Times said it was, " ... a sad Christmas, but his memory will be treasured by many thousands."

Why am I, 69 years later, recalling this man and his death?

Because I own an elderly building — the Theilman Building — at 703 West St. Germain Street. When the building was built in 1895, J.D. Sullivan practiced law from its second floor for 10 years.

You've got a Mickey Mantle rookie card, a Victorian chair or vintage Dr Pepper sign? Heck, I've got a whole building that spans three centuries! (So do you, actually.) But I didn't much appreciate it — do you? — until ...

I have a photograph of the building when it was new; it shows a wooden sign that says, "Law Office, Sullivan" between two of the upstairs windows. One day I was on Germain staring up at my historic possession and I noticed two bent nails extending out from the bricks — in the same place the sign had been.

When J.D. Sullivan left the building, did one of the Theilman brothers just open one of the windows, reach out with a crow bar

> **"I've got a whole building that spans three centuries!"**

and get it all down except those two nails? Have they been there for a quarter century, then a world war, a Great Depression, another world war and then my lifetime to date?

Until ...

Until I was walking past the Lahr Building at Sixth and Germain. Tom Grones and Dan Rudningen have renovated it to house their company GeoComm, and what they've done is impressive. And they have included an original touch. They've identified the building's historic tenants with 28 second-floor window decals and first floor signage.

It's imaginative. Give yourself a treat as another year comes to a close; get Auntie Tilda out of the senior care center and take her and the kids to downtown to read the Lahr building.

Yes, I said, "Read the building."

My guess is stories of Christmas past will flow like nog as your oldest passenger is stimulated to relive the past! Heck, even I remember

Stevenson's Department Store, 1935-84, and Tra-Clare Beauty Salon, 1947-94. But who was Cecilia Fox-Dressmaker, 1906? Was she pretty? How cool was Henry's Corner Drug Store, 1914-27?

The GeoComm building spurred me to the same — but different— with my building. Off I went to the Great River Regional Library, the Stearns History Museum and to an attorney. (You ever try to read an abstract?)

I am caught up in writing the definitive history of my building; so much so that I'm spending waaaay too much time on this.

An interesting note, St Cloud's Journal Press reported Feb. 28, 1895) that "Plans for the new building ... are already made ... and the new firm will occupy their new store about July 1st."

Apparently in that "primitive" time, it was to be expected that a wood-frame building could be razed and a two-story brick building constructed on the same spot in four months!

My purpose for writing this is two-fold. One, I encourage anyone else to follow the lead shown with the fine new GeoComm/Lahr building.

But I also would like any help I can get with my project: Is anybody left out there who knows anything about any of my building's former tenants, including the following people?

Leonard Theilman, sons Frank and George, and so on. Leonard constructed the building and his hardware store occupied it until 1947.

Charles Metzroth. He left the pioneer Metzroth merchandising firm and went into real estate, a tenant from 1912 to 1933. I bought the building from his grandchildren.

Mark Thelen

Lorenzo Rochol (1908-33), county school superintendent, city treasurer and city finance commissioner.

Joseph Satory (1906-16), a dentist.

A. N. Lengas, owned Ideal Novelty (photographic) Studio, 1908.

William J. (Billy) Alden, 1904-06, was "Chief Justice of St Cloud," the April 15, 1932, Times reports.

Eri Salter, apparently this guy lived up there during the first world war.

Thomas Urbaniak, 1904, a tailor.

Whoever operated "Artcraft Studio" in the late 1940s.

I've got the building for a little while. As did they. I want to preserve it, in case anyone cares, years from now.

Happy holidays.

Originally published on 12.27.2002
Copyright *St. Cloud Times*

Center for Hope, Healing project is a good place to start

I wish I were a famous movie star, married to a wonderful woman and living in the Hollywood Hills. Oh well, one out of three ain't bad. But I do wish I were more like, say, Michael Douglas, don't you? Sure you do.

Douglas has got it all. And why? Because he said, "Greed is good" in the movie "Wall Street." The line created a buzz, his fame grew and the movie and Douglas made box-office mega-bucks.

Three words, alliteration and some shock value. Simple.

Well, two can play the same game: "Guilt is good."

What, you may ask, is this all about? Well, I needed to hook you into this column and I needed a jaunty star-studded beginning because this column is about guilt and about getting out your checkbook.

> **"I needed a jaunty star-studded beginning."**

You try to hold your readers with that mission in mind.

The problem with guilt is it often serves no productive purpose; it is so often kindled by something that cannot be undone. It only bums one out. Guilt is, however, good when three conditions are met:

You are not personally responsible for the guilt-inducing horror.

The guilt motivates you to corrective action.

Your action actually fixes the problem.

But how often are those conditions present? Well, BINGO! We've got such a situation right now, right here.

We are on the threshold of fixing the problem of homelessness in Central Minnesota, and if you help, you won't have to feel guilty about it anymore. You will still, of course, have to deal with world hunger and that little cheating episode of yours, be it marital or be it sophomoric geometry.

But first a word about the problem and how it conjures guilt.

Each cold winter night when our conscientious northern-clime heads hit our pillows, two phenomena occur. We experience great relief that we and ours are in and warm. And we also shudder (that's the guilt working) because we know others are not. (I hope the day this column is printed, it's 20 below zero because the effect on readers will be so much more visceral.)

What are we to do? Go find a few of these people and invite them in? That is as insufficient as it is unlikely, for even if we did, more would remain out there.

Here's the deal. We can help build a brand new — and adequate — homeless shelter here in Central Minnesota. And — make no mistake — it will be for Central Minnesotans. Away goes that guilt, to be replaced with a warming, soothing sense of well-being.

Now, if there are two things about as off-putting as guilt, they are facts and details. Don't you just hate facts and details? Sure you do.

But you might like these: Quietly, for several years, volunteers have been laying the groundwork to build a new shelter for homeless people.

STEP UP, HELP SOLVE HOMELESSNESS

And so as not to sully the purity of my motives, I disclose that I have been
among those volunteers. In addition, I also want you to know my advertising business - a few years ago - provided this project with a
few services for minimal compensation; that is, the charges barely
covered costs.

That done, let's get back to curing homelessness.

This project already has a name, "The Center for Hope and Healing." Nice
name. It will be very, very adequate. Its price tag is $5 million, but the
campaign to build it is
off to a great start. A
site already has been
arranged on the VA
Medical Center

66Guilt is good. **99**

grounds, and a large grant of money from the Federal Home Loan Bank
has been announced. The facility will have 90-beds of emergency shelter
and 15 units of transitional housing.

Bear this in mind: 85 percent of those using the local Salvation Army
shelter are individuals and families (and families) from Central
Minnesota. About 90 percent work (!) and 38 percent are American
armed services veterans.

I have chosen to devote a column to this good cause because it has some
singularity about it: It addresses a contemporary in-the-news problem.

It is not an annual eleemosynary appeal. It is large. It is tangible. That is, it
will become a permanent part of our landscape. It is likely to succeed; it is
off to a good start and has a broad base of support.

Here's where this column starts to gain true quality; I'm stepping aside to draw upon real writing talent. May he succeed where I may have fallen short. Let's give it up, guys and gals, for Charles Dickens.

(Thunderous applause)

"Chuck, what have you for us today?"

"Thanks, Mark. Hey great to be here in St Cloud. Love your river, folks. It isn't the Thames, but it's not bad."

(Audience chuckles good-naturedly.)

"But seriously, folks, remember when I was scaring the crap out of Scroogey with those three ghosts? Remember the second one? When I brought the "yellow, meager" kids out from his robe? Give a listen.

" 'Have they no refuge or resource?' said Scrooge.

'Are there no prisons?' said the Spirit, turning on him for the last time with his own words. 'Are there no workhouses?'

The bell struck twelve."

Originally published on 1.24.2003
Copyright *St. Cloud Times*

Writer's note: Wherever the words "employees" and "workers" appear in this column, substitute them with "programs" and you have an equally worthy second column, free!

How would you like it if any future salary increases you get were to be wiped out because they would be taxed at the rate of 100 percent? Loathsome, eh?

Balancing the budget is required by the state Constitution. "I will do it without raising taxes," says the man you and I elected governor. Some of you don't agree that he can, and others believe he should. I am, of course, your neutral observer/reporter.

Since the election, Gov. Tim Pawlenty has submitted his budget proposal, part of which is "No wage increases for government employees."

Now I ask you, isn't that the same as giving them raises but with a tax increase imposed at 100 percent on those raises? If it is different, it is only slightly so.

Here is a bonus thought: Are not state college tuition increases, in effect, tax increases on those paying tuition?

The punch line

So why would such an idea be offered by our youthful governor and expected to "fly" with good Minnesotans?

Because we don't like government and by extension, its workers.

"Close enough for government work." Ha ha. "Can the government do anything right?" He he. "The other day I saw some highway guys filling in a pothole. There were two big trucks and seven guys standing around watching one guy carry a spade of asphalt." Geez.

You've heard similar conversations.

At a recent meeting, one of my fellow private enterprisers offered one of those government-workers-are-so-lazy-stupid-or-inefficient comments. He he.

This comment was then reinforced by another. Hardy, har. And this general agreement occurred despite — or maybe because — three of the dozen or so meeting participants were government administrators. But we were just kidding. He he. And expecting them to be good sports. The three smiled a bit painfully and no doubt hoped the meeting would quickly return to the agenda.

Yes, it seems bashing government employees is common and that reducing the deficit via cuts in which a burden falls more heavily to them goes beyond painful necessity. It goes beyond acceptable.

"Can the government do anything right?"

You know what I hear? I hear glee. For some, this is a long-awaited victory without alloy!

But be careful. This country did not invent, nor are its citizens in sole possession of that thing called self-interest or personal initiative. That trait is found across the globe, and it has been forever thus. Yet, it is generally cited as the characteristic that has made the United States' economic engine the mighty power it is.

What has made this country wealthy (although irregularly so), is the partnership between government and personal drive. Too little government equals anarchy and chaos. Too much government stifles ambition. We in the United States for centuries seem to have magically struck a balance. And we had better keep it!

Be wary

Do we really despise government workers? In the abstract, yes. But with a little thought, when we get down to specifics, we actually appreciate them — very much. To illustrate:

How do you feel about the local police and firefighters? They work for the government.

Wake up after a stormy winter night and off we go on cleared streets. Not bad for government work, huh?

School teachers? Think of your favorite when you were younger, or think of the one or six who motivated your little child to go skipping to the bus stop.

Prison guards? I'd be scared to do what they do.

Government horticulturists? When gunk starts spreading on your berry bush, who ya gonna call?

And how about our parks? Always delightful. Conceived by government people, executed by other government employees, these are an orchestra of flowers, trees, ponds, benches, picnic tables and trails.

Do you like smallpox? Governments wiped it out and it will be government that will respond to terrorists with viral attack in mind.

War on milfoil? Government.

Funny uncle Harry still with us because of his pacemaker? Medtronics would not exist today had not the University of Minnesota invented the gadget.

And then there is a large collection of private efforts that get funding through government contracts. For example,

> **"When gunk starts spreading on your berry bush, who ya gonna call?"**

private school bus companies. Have you received an invoice lately? Why not? Catholic Charities? Catholic or not, you've got to appreciate their work. A large chunk of that revenue comes via government contract.

And on and on.

Now, don't get me wrong, I'm sure some state budget items should be reduced or made more efficient. But a lot of tax-paying government workers are about to be unemployed with the remaining having greater stress and heavier workloads.

But I have detected some glee, some sense of triumph in some circles now that government is about to be slashed. I think it inappropriate. A little thought should reveal that. However needed, solving this massive deficit is not about glee. It is about glum. You'll see.

Until lawmakers pass the concealed handgun law, I continue to be limited in my ability to defend myself and you may confidently continue to criticize my column.

Originally published on 2.28.2003
Copyright *St. Cloud Times*

Local radio show plays into hands of area's struggling reputation

I don't know them personally. It's their on-air personalities I want stopped. Not just because I don't like their hate-filled spew, but because they menace our community.

Yes, I have an ox to grind.

It's the local radio show "Hot Talk with the Ox." "The Ox" is Dan. He has a verbal lap dog, Don. I'd call him "the cowardly Lyon" if only I were so clever.

They talk as bullies and, as such, cowards. They speak ignorance in drag as arrogance. They waste talent consorting with the comfortable and afflicting the uncomfortable, all the while, slavishly agreeing with each other, "egg-zackt-ly."

I'm not going to tell you their station or day part, because I don't want to add to their tiny audience.

Arbitron figures indicate they have just 200 listeners during an average quarter hour. Not 1,000, not 10,000. Two hundred! Another station in the same broadcast group has nine times that number.

Ridiculous things

On the show, they select topics while squinting through jade-colored glasses, then agree with each other that some one, some thing or some process is ridiculous. But only when there is no one in the studio to counter their attacks.

When someone is present, they are polite — though cloying — and productive interviewers. Most of the time, though, they are free to enjoy picking on less fortunate citizens. On less employed and less comfortable neighbors.

And on every show, they deride issues of human harmony among diverse groups.

I can just hear them, "Can you believe this crap?" or "These people seem to think ..." Simpleton responses.

> **"Yes, I have an ox to grind."**

Their pap causes and encourages the worst in society. (Aside to Dan and Don, such relentless anger almost always masks serious unresolved personal issues. Consider professional counseling.)

Be more specific?

OK. On two occasions I heard them use the term "homos" derisively. It seemed offensive to me so I checked. It is.

And I called the show and pointed this out to them — politely, I swear — and also said, "and so I'm asking you not to use that term anymore."

I was told, "shut up" and was cut off.

But also, early this month I heard something very close to this:

"So caller, your fourth gay-and-lesbian-awareness question is: A motel in Stickett, Indiana, offers a special weekend package for homosexual couples. True or False.

"And by the way, (I am still quoting them) the motel is called the Stickett Inn."

As if it were rollicking good cheer. As if it were not snide and not intended to be harmful.

Local radio, local people! It embarrasses me to repeat it.

That's just one example. They are relentless in their obnoxious condescension and superiority — day after day. We live in vulgar times, so that alone probably won't bring them down.

But this could: The morning that was aired, a member of our St Cloud City Council was not just a guest, he was a guest host! He did not actively participate in that unfunny bit; he may not even have been aware of it. I'm told it was on tape.

But while the council member was not involved in the gay bashing, neither did he get up and walk out in protest. He is a regular on the show. Part of the show. He is not there just to report on city government.

His participation is not unique. Many other show regulars also are elected officials — and other eminences —

> **"I was told, "shut up" and was cut off. "**

whose participation ranges from single-event, straight reportage (I was once a guest on the show) to frequent chummy, clubby "appearances."

And almost all, I am sure, know of the show's usual pathological tenor.

At-risk career

Now, if any of you who are guests don't see eye-to-eye with me about these two mirthy lads, consider how you are putting your careers and reputations at risk.

These are two loose cannons, and you don't know what they are going to say next — and next to your guest shot.

Just imagine the impact and accompanying embarrassment had my topic — and your name — been featured by a Twin Cities medium and presented as the latest chapter of St Cloud's hotbed-of-intolerance saga. How embarrassing and damaging to you and this metropolitan area. Whether you agree with me or not.

I am cautioning future guests to stay away from the show. You can no longer plead ignorance. Your participation in the show could be viewed as complicity. Bigotry by association.

Here's another problem: The one named Don also is a radio announcer for St Cloud State University hockey games. I'm thinking the university has not yet made the connection, and I am guessing he is not an employee of the university but of the radio company that contracts with it.

I am hoping the parties of the first- and second-part are, as we read, racing each other to the phone to fix it. St. Cloud State does not need any more insensitive-to-diversity taint.

We in "White Cloud" have suffered more than our share of human rights bruises.

So now let us imagine some people driving into our towns searching for the answer to this question: Does this community 'do unto others' with kindness and decency?

They tune their radio to a local station and hear the ridiculing, guffawing and hoo-hawing as I have described. Then they hear this "... and right after the break we'll be talking to Community Leader So and So about ..."

Would they dig deeper for their answer? Would they consider relocating their family to our community? Would they wish to move a business here?

Would you?

Originally published on 3.28.2003
Copyright *St. Cloud Times*

If I do say so myself, I think I've got a pretty good idea: Let us apply a poultice of good old American greenbacks on a community wound. Moola.

To set the mood as you read this column, go to your home music library, locate your "ABBA's Golden Greats" CD and play their big hit, "Money, Money, Money," in which they promise that it is "always sunny, in a rich man's world."

When The Mediterranean Cafe in downtown St. Cloud was vandalized, it was done by cowards who painted hateful recommendations around the restaurant's alley entrance.

It is important to know that the ownership and management of The Mediterranean are people who have moved here from Somalia. The manager, Abdi Ali Mohamed, left his homeland because of "10 years of war" in his country. Ironic, isn't it?

The response from Abdi regarding the episode: "I know it is not the majority who feel that way."

Some portions of our community responded to the incident with support. They recommended encouraging notes be sent to the people at the restaurant. So notes were sent and posted in the restaurant. Excellent.

St. Cloud's Downtown Council sent out an appeal for vigilant volunteers to keep an eye on the place. Excellent.

Try the goat

My response? I gave them some money. Why? Because it's a restaurant and I ate there. Good food. Lots of it. I didn't forget the tip.

From the menu, I chose the goat! First time in my life. Later, friends said, "GOAT?!?" I said, "It was good, and how's that different than lamb?" But hey, this is not your average American restaurant. This is your average Somalia-in-America restaurant. Mideast meets Midwest. Try the goat; you can handle it.

It was a nice dining experience and an unusual one by Central Minnesota standards. Bring the kids, you'll thrive.

❝Try the goat. ❞

Or try the Marinated Curried Chicken with spices, green peppers and tomatoes. Or the steak. Each is served with a side dish (I had the rice, next time the pasta) and a lettuce salad. If your taste buds are not very adventurous, don't worry, neither are mine. I found the food very tasty. And did I say there was lots of it?

The atmosphere? A minimalist middle American style with a few exotic touches on the wall. You will feel right at home. Well, kind of. Remember, while they are people who speak excellent English, they do have an unfamiliar accent. The conversation was part of the experience: I kept asking my waiter to repeat, and he patiently kept repeating. Part of the fun.

Hey, good food and a good broadening experience. You can handle it.

Gift of commerce

So, here's what I want us to do. Let's give these folks the greatest gift one can give a newcomer to our town: commerce. Go eat there. Let us let them pocket some of our money. I believe there is nothing else we can do to make them feel so genuinely and thoroughly welcome.

Churches, read this request from the pulpit right after the beatitudes.

Liberals and progressives, put your money where your mouths are, so to speak.

Conservatives, let's give these people a lesson in the glory of the American free enterprise system. Show 'em what economic freedom is all about.

Hmmm, let's see, what else we can do? Hey, Rotarians, hold one of your weekly meetings there. "That'll be 36 for lunch, please!" Has any service club asked them to join? Oh, you have, how was I to know? You haven't? Why not?

Accounting firms? Law firms? Wonder if they could use a little help figuring out our system?

How about one of our restaurant supply firms? Pay a visit and see what you might offer to help.

> **❝Yup, you go in and enjoy a big meal. ❞**

What if this fledgling enterprise became a huge American success story? I see a movie deal coming: "Sunny Skies Come to a Cloudy Town." Denzel Washington as Abdi. Real inspiring stuff. Richard Dreyfuss could play me! Sorry, got carried away with a vision of Central Minnesota as a font of kindness, helpfulness and harmony.

Now let's see, what can I do? I own an ad agency. Hmmmm. I've got it! We'll produce that proven classic of American restaurant marketing, a promotional coupon! Only, let's throw in an imaginative twist: Instead of a Dollar Off, let's make it a Dollar On!

Yup, you go in and enjoy a big meal, go to the register, hand them the money (don't forget the tip) and then hand them the "Dollar On" coupon. They say, "That'll be another dollar please."

You say, "Thank you very much. There you are."

You see, the idea here is not to save you money. It is to make them money.

Thus, everyone at the Mediterranean Restaurant at 815 St. Germain feels viable and that they are a welcome in our community. No reservations needed.

Originally published on 4.25.2003
Copyright *St. Cloud Times*

Why do you live in St. Cloud? You write the next column

Vacations are often the occasions of troublesome thoughts. Edinburgh, Scotland sure was. It was prompting me to say, "I could live here." And that's troublesome because to continue that thinking would mean closing up one's life — serious stuff. But then, so is staying the course, living as one has always lived, dutifully waiting for the big move — heaven.

On the flight home from Scotland, chatting with strangers while thwarting transatlantic clots forming in our legs and booking passage to our lungs, I heard this more than once, "Oh, St. Cloud, that's a nice place."

Have you ever heard that? Sure you have.

Sometimes I ask back, "So, what do you think is nice about it?" Then they say, "Oh I don't know, I've just heard it's nice." or "Why, don't you like it?" Or often I hear, "Well, isn't it growing?" These are not answers.

I guess maybe they are just being polite, you know, making conversation. I should learn to be a little more pleasant and just kind of go with the flow. I'll work on that.

> **"I should learn to be a little more pleasant."**

Why move here?

But sometimes I hear comments that simply must have more content than aimless chit-chat. "Well, we're from Vermont but decided we would rather live in St. Cloud, so we moved."

"You moved here? Why!?!" Not the "Were-you-completely-off-your-rocker" why. More like the "Please, I need to know; I'm living my entire and only life here and I am wondering if there isn't something more" kind of why.

These people had a choice. Indeed they had overcome inertia. They relocated a thousand miles to get here. Here! Why here? "We had moved to Santa Barbara (!) for five years but we decided to move back."

Why?

"Oh, I don't know; I went to State and just kind of liked the town."

Why?

"I don't know, Jennifer and I met at The Red Carpet and we just wanted to come back?"

Why? Why? Why!?!

"Hey, are you all right? Your hands are shaky and your knees are weak. You can't seem to stand on your own two feet."

Scenic places

LaCrosse, Wis., is cool. Seems to be a lot like St. Cloud except one or two quanta more scenic. Many surviving mansions in impeccable, honored condition. Bluffs including the "Grand daddy" of them all.

Duluth! Wow! Been to the boardwalk lately? That big ship? The lift bridge? The largest fresh water lake in the world. Elevation. They have had legislators who built careers gleefully bringing bacon home to their folks. Not like some of ours who oppose everything new and fabulous; burdened, conflicted and frozen by vague and regressive "principles."

Hey, loosen up and show us the money! Too late now, I guess.

Many places have mountains. We have a single slope and what do we do with it? Put dead people in it. So we can keep an eye on them. In case they get any ideas about finally being rid of life and starting to have some fun. Heavens.

No ocean. No desert. No hang gliding. No world's largest statue of a blue gill or a chicken. No world's largest anything. Even tiny towns have those things. New York Mills has a "Think Off." Wish I'd thought of that.

> **"Put dead people in it."**

What's there to do?

And what's to do around here? Let's see: 1. Shop. 2. Go out to eat. 3. Go to a movie. That's about all.

We almost had an events center. But the electorate said, "What do we want that for?" To do stuff, I should have thought. But noooooo.

Readers, can't you tell I'm having a little crisis here? I, who have so often used this very columnar space to laud these communities and their peoples, need your help. Please tell me what you think is so great about this town. And by this town I mean Saint Waite Sarpark.

Don't mention things like, "Oh, the people are friendly" or "The schools, I like the schools." Lots of places have friendly people and good schools.

Folks, you write the next column; I'm just not up to it. Reassure me.

Tell me what's so great about this area. What's special. Or, tell me what we should have and then we'd be cool. If I get sufficient response, I'll do a follow-up column.

And don't tell me that our compelling charm is that this locale is marvelously adequate and delightfully nonawful. I've already thought of it. And I don't think I'm alone in my thinking.

Originally published on 5.23.2003
Copyright *St. Cloud Times*

Strong opinions sometimes beget unthinkable acts

Have you noticed that things are getting a little — I don't know — weird?

Do you have an opinion about (locally) thousands of Somalis having moved here, (stately) Tim Pawlenty's budget without its taxes and with its social services cuts, and (nationally) our recent Iraq war with and without its weapons of mass destruction?

I'll bet you have some strong thoughts about each. I'll also bet you carefully choose when to express them because to raise the issues could result in some conversational friction.

Liberals, Muslims, the Christian right, illegal aliens, GLBT, the rich, welfare cheats, Toms Daschle and DeLay, oil people, the French, weapons of mass destruction, tax and spenders, talk show crabs and Native American fishing rights. Thus far, we have maintained domestic tranquility, but on so many issues, we are more deeply divided than I have seen in my lifetime.

> **"Now back to our depressing essay."**

Even worse

What if things get worse? A further worsening economy, another two or three little wars following another domestic terror attack or two, disruptive rallies by the poor and unemployed, an assassination perhaps.

People and groups have been known to do some pretty awful things when stressed. Burning witches. Holding inquisitions. That sort of thing. Excessive hockey jubilation. Powder puff football hazing. The Holocaust. That sort of stuff.

But first this message to help you plan your summer travel: "Later this summer a new attraction will be opening in Duluth. Yes, the city that boasts such a great lake and so much more ... is getting ready to offer you a new attraction: the Clayton, Jackson, McGhie Memorial. Plan to see it; bring the whole family."

Now back to our depressing essay.

Every discussion I have ever heard about atrocities — by groups — has always been from a certain point of view. How ever could they have done such a thing? Someone else, somewhere else, some other time. Those people must surely have been different than us. We could never do such a thing. We are comforted that these events were long ago and far away.

But isn't the better question, "Could we do something really shameful?" Us and soon?

Maybe it's time some of us in Central Minnesota have a serious talk about rounding up some of our neighbors, entire families, and taking them just outside of town and doing — well — doing something awful.

There, I've even shocked myself.

So let's take a deep breath and reread that last paragraph and make sure that I didn't write about actually doing something; I wrote about talking about doing it.

That's a big difference.

And let's have this talk so that we may avoid the actuality of such — ah, umh — unpleasantness.

What would it take to allow us, to seem to require us to commit mayhem? And perhaps in the name of justice or to "preserve order" or to "protect our security."

We live in a country I increasingly do not understand. I am beginning to fear us!

Many readers, some angrily, have stopped reading this essay. But some of you are wide-eyed.

See? Divisions.

Looking back

In 1941, the Nazis invaded the northeastern Polish town of Jedwabne. They herded 1,600 townspeople — men, women and children — into a barn and burned it and them.

Or so the good Jedwabnians believed for 60 years. One part of the story, however, was not true. It wasn't the Nazis, it was the

> **"There, I've even shocked myself."**

Jedwabnians themselves who did the herding and burning. Neighbors, blaming the Nazis, killed their neighbors. Today's Jedwabnian knows it was mommy and daddy.

Otherwise — good people under not — uncommon circumstances can collectively open a door of mass murder, close it very quickly, and go back to family picnics, church gatherings and work. Probably never to speak of it again.

When the Oklahoma bombing news broke, I was in a client meeting. One of us said, "It was the Arabs." No one protested this assertion, though it had no basis. It was two really white guys. Several years later, we had Sept. 11. So, he was right after all, huh?

Remember family gatherings during the Vietnam era? That was not so long ago and not at all far away. It's still a good topic to avoid.

Is a Central Minnesota "incident" possible? How? Raise the question. I guarantee a lively discussion at your next book group, social science class, service club lunch or prayer breakfast. Can you handle it?

Not could it happen here? But how could it happen here?

Now, for our closing announcement:

"So folks, remember to stop in friendly Duluth, our good neighbor to the north where in 1920, a woman falsely accused three young men of raping her.

Then, thousands of Duluthians dangled them from a downtown lamppost. These three have contributed their names to Duluth's newest attraction: the Clayton, Jackson, McGhie Memorial."

Originally published on 6.27.2003
Copyright *St. Cloud Times*

Americans can govern themselves

Responsible citizens won't pay any taxes to government when I'm president

I was going to run for only the governorship, but I am a person of generous spirit, so why not extend the benefits to all Americans?

Yes, the rumors are true. I'm also running for president!

Historians will want to know, so Albany, get busy. Choosing a presidential library site is not easy.

How did my decision to seek — strike that, achieve — public office come about? It was sudden, and here's how it happened:

> **"But what if I get pregnant?"**

Earlier this month I received my first paycheck of the new Gov. Tim Pawlenty/President Bush golden age. Shocker; money was still being withheld! I went to my payroll administrator, Becky, and said, "Hey, what's with this? Get with the program: No more taxes!" I was berserk.

She was calm as she said, "That's 'No new taxes.' "

Right there in that instant was found the germ of my dual candidacy. I noted my (mistaken) joy at no more taxes and my (appropriate) ennui with no new taxes. I decided, No more taxes is better! Pawlenty and Bush were mere kindlers of the bonfire of the idea that will sweep me into office(s).

The lynch pin of "No more taxes" is "no more government." Simple, isn't it? But some readers may wonder what of the goods and services offered via governments?

Gone. And good riddance. Let's select a few for elucidation.

Let's start with an easy one. Government social welfare programs will once and for all be ended. All of them will be replaced with personal responsibility. You believe in personal responsibility, don't you?

Elderly, frail parents can move in with their children. Teen-age sex and its accompanying welfare babies? No more will be heard, "Come on, baby." "But what if I get pregnant?" "Don't worry, baby; the government will help out." "Oh, OK."

See? Personal responsibility.

What about police? Who knows better how "to protect and to serve" than we the citizenry, now empowered to carry all the law enforcement that's needed — personal handguns? I trust Americans to do what's right with those guns. Yes, America will be a nation of 260 million cops! Talk about feeling safe.

Courts? No more government means no more courts. No courts means no attorneys. All disputes will be soothed via average, hard-working citizens talking things over and coming to a reasonable decision. And again, of course, backed by the full knowledge that both parties are trained in the use of nearby firearms.

Fire departments. We only need them because we think we need them. Hey, how many of you have ever had a fire? Nobody I know. And you want to know why? Because responsible citizens remove oily rags from stairwells and inspect their wiring regularly without the government telling them. Those who don't probably will now start to do so, knowing that the government isn't going to bail them out with all those expensive trucks, endangering brave men and women to put out their flames of irresponsibility.

Highways? Toll roads have a glorious history of success in America. Can't afford to pay tolls? Then maybe you can't afford to drive. Maybe you never could! Why make me pay for your trips to get your doggie groomed?

Schools? That's the easiest of all. Private schools — religious and otherwise — and home schooling, too. Government schools have always meant

> **"Why make me pay for your trips to get your doggie groomed?"**

government control and rules. And in the "Era Called Thelen," you can teach any dang thing you want. Anything. Moon is made of blue cheese? Teach away. Man evolved from apes? Ha ha, go ahead. Intentionally throwing in wacky ideas keeps kids on their intellectual toes, thinking critically.

National defense? You thought this would be a hard one, didn't you? It's not. First, the timid National Rifle Association needs to get off their cold dead butts and catch up with the Thelen Administration. It thinks it is so cool insuring your right to carry dinky little side arms and shotguns. What about bazookas? What about shoulder-launched rockets? Let's see someone menace our fruited plains and planes when every citizen is packing big-league heat, when every family's hum-vee and jeep is equipped the way nature intended.

Foreign wars? Let's make them profit centers. Let's privatize the armed forces and make their work hearken to the old bottom line. Our current Iraq involvement serves as an excellent prototype. Vice President Dick Cheney's former firm, Halliburton, has been awarded construction contracts there amounting to almost half a billion dollars.

Congressman Henry Waxman (a Democrat of course) from California (it figures) has questioned our U.S. Army about these contracts, which, he said, allow "Halliburton to profit from virtually every phase of the war."

As if that is a bad thing!?! He just doesn't get it.

Does all this seem revolutionary? It isn't. I'm not that smart. All I've done is apply some guts and grit and extend our current enlightened socio-econo-politico thought to its logical terminus. Our current leaders, you see, stop short. They are - I hate to say this - timid. It is up to all of you and me to allow America to reach full bloom.

Originally published on 7.25.2003
Copyright *St. Cloud Times*

Kids want advice, and so do I

Soon I will speak to a gymnasium full of high-schoolers for 'career days'

I'm in a real pickle. Help! I am to speak at a "career days" event at Holdingford High School this October. I have to relate to young people for the better part of an hour! It's an important job. I fear I'm not up to it.

Why me? I don't know. Maybe they got me mixed up with someone else. Maybe they thought I was Mark Sakry or somebody. (He'd have been good.) Why didn't I just say no?

Imagine the scene: Young people herded into the gymnasium to listen to some guy tell them what to do with the rest of their lives. They deserve better than, "Listen to your parents and teachers ... blah, blah ... You can be anything you dream ... blah, blah ... Study hard and don't have sex."

Geez, I'm going to be awful. They're going to hate me.

Several administrators will probably be asked to resign over it. Holdingford, it's not too late to get out of it. Holdingford parents, don't you care about your youngsters?

So what am I going to do? Well, I am going to show up and do the best I can because that's one

"Hey, now we're cooking."

thing my dad always told me — "When you say you're going to do something, you do it." Hey, that's good advice; I'll tell them that.

Career success guidepost No. 1: When you agree to do something, you do it. Hey, now we're cooking. How much time does that take up?

Hey, I just thought of another thing.

Career success guidepost No. 2: Buy a good umbrella! That will use up some time, especially if I tell them why. What looks sillier than an otherwise sharp-looking career tracker, on-the-rise, haplessly foundering in the rain under a damaged, dinky umbrella? Your power clothes get drenched from the shoulders down, and you uncooly scurry under cheap tissue you call an umbrella.

Not so for our current Holdingford High student, future job holder. Success-advantaged with my good counsel, the student can confidently stride beneath a tent-diametered, titanium-sparred beauty that shouts, "A man or woman prepared. Big umbrella, big career!"

Students, for less than $100 you can be a person of some distinction, a person who seems to have seen much and forgotten little. You will make an impression equivalent to a Cadillac Encapsilade, which cost a thousand times as much.

Does it surprise you to know that I possess such an umbrella?

There, two things to tell the youngsters at Holdingford High. I fear it is not enough so I need your help.

Readers, what would you say to young people? What is the best advice you have ever been given? What is the worst? Yes, that's it. Let's deal in superlatives. Don't forget that there is something in it for you. These Holdingford Huskers are all that stand between us and the looming Social Security insolvency.

Maybe, with our collective wisdom and experience, we'll be great.

Here is what I don't want. I don't want platitudes similar to "You can be anything you believe you can be." No you can't. I want specifics. Like my terrific umbrella tenet. Like the guy in "The Graduate" who told Dustin Hoffman, "plastics."

Now the thing I don't like about "plastics" is that it is one word. Too short.

"Big umbrella, big career!"

Remember, I've got almost an hour.

I also don't want sanctimonious. Kids see right through sanctimonious.

I don't want religious stuff either because this is a public school and I don't want to get arrested. Besides, it's not my style.

Similarly, I don't want any champion athlete stories. As a matter of fact, I hate inspirational stuff of any kind.

I like practical stuff. What do you think they ought to do? What do you think they ought not do?

And it doesn't have to directly relate to careers. Many other aspects of one's life impact one's job success.

If you would like to share your ideas, my e-mail address is at the end of this column. Or, those of you who are up to it, can go to the usual spot on the Times Web site. I'll be checking "Story Chat" all day with hope in my soul.

Before I close, you must know that not one single young person is

NOW WHAT'S HE TALKING ABOUT?

actually going to buy a deluxe umbrella. So you must buy it for them.

I'm saying it because it's true. We both know young people need a good umbrella. It's part of work, the thing that will keep them going. If their plane leaves Holdingford and a fine umbrella is not with them, you'll regret it. Maybe not today. Maybe not tomorrow, but soon and for the rest of your life.

Originally published on 8.22.2003
Copyright *St. Cloud Times*

What could we do if we spent the money here instead of Iraq?

"A billion here, a billion there, and pretty soon you're talking about real money." —*Sen. Everett Dirksen 1896-1969*

I'd like to give $1 million dollars to help provide for the homeless and for food shelves in each of our tri-counties. I know it would really come in handy. But then, Morrison County would get in a snit, so we better make sure they get $1 million, too. Naturally, we can't keep that sort of thing quiet so we better just do it in all of Minnesota's counties.

That comes to $87,000,000 because Minnesota has 87 counties.

Similarly, let's give our state's schools the same amount. Yeah, good idea; another $87,000,000.

Let's see, what else? How about awarding 500 scholarships worth $2,000 each in every county. That's 43,500 state scholarships.

> **"We also serve who worry."**

Now let's give 1,000 teachers in each county $1,000 bonuses. That's 87,000 Minnesota teachers saying, "Sure beats an apple."

Talk about supporting our troops, let's also fund the equipment needs for our local homeland security troops (such as police and fire).

Then let's give $1 million to Catholic Charities and Lutheran Social Services; they have to split it, though. And $1 million to the Sexual Assault Center and the Woman House Shelter. And similarly around the state.

I don't doubt this column might be getting a tad tedious for you. That's just too bad because we've got work to do and a point to be made. So let's just "suck it up."

But why should those less fortunate have all the fun? Hey, let's all live a little by randomly giving away 5,800 new cars to Minnesota families and building 10 $8.7 million community centers across the state.

Then let's give everybody in the state $25 for anything. That means a family of four gets $100! Everybody. No restrictions. You want hot dogs, a new Bible or some ammo, go ahead.

OK, I'm pooped. I just fantastically handed out $87,000,000 10 times. Now, if I just had the patience and column space to list 10 more ways (including preschool programs, help for the elderly and beer giveaways) to spend $87,000,000, that would be 20.

Now let's be fair and do the same thing in all 49 other states. Here goes:

Alabama? They get 20 times $87,000,000. Alaska? Same deal. And on and on and on we go to Massachusetts and Michigan. And on and on through Oregon and Tennessee until we arrive at the end of the alphabet with Wyoming.

That's right. Twenty times $87,000,000 times 50 states, which comes to $87 billion.

Each and every state gets $1,740,000,000.

Nationally, we've given out 2,175,000 scholarships, provided 4,350,000 teachers with bonuses, delighted 290,000 families with a brand new car, sent checks to all Americans totalling $4.35 billion and built 500 community recreation centers. And a whole bunch of other stuff. A whole bunch.

"But that's more than the federal government spent on highways, education and parks — combined!!" you say.

Yes, and it also is the same amount President Bush requested to wage the war in Iraq, in addition to the $79 billion he already had gotten.

And we are spending that money on a truly fat "maybe." When we spend $176,000,000,000, shouldn't it be on a "for sure"?

The only thing that is not a maybe is we are there and no one is saying how and when we are going to get out.

What are we going to do? Not supply our troops? Unthinkable. We cannot leave, and we cannot accomplish the mission. Reminds me of ... it reminds me of ... I can't say it.

> **66** You want hot dogs, a new Bible or some ammo, go ahead. **99**

Here's another thing. Where's the money going to come from? Are we going to run a tab, or is Bush going to ask to raise taxes? The former means our kids pay and he cannot do the latter. Remember, "Read my lips?"

All this against next year's deficit of $500 billion and every year into the guessable future.

Aren't you scared about the continuing financial integrity of this country? That is, this nation's continuing security?

We also serve who worry.

Defining $87 billion

If each dollar sign below represented $1,000, well over 50,000 pages of this book would be needed to contain enough dollar signs to equal $87 billion.

Originally published on 9.26.2003

Copyright *St. Cloud Times*

$$\$$
$$

Know the details to make an informed vote or have faith

I have no idea what I'm talking about in this column. I am in waaaay over my head. This levy stuff is so complicated. But I have to make some sense of it because I am going to have to decide the matter because I vote.

Chatting with a smart colleague, we noticed the nifty "Levyes" lawn signs, the ones with the pencil and that shared "Y." I spoke admiringly of its graphic design.

He said he was not capable of an objective opinion about the sign because it promotes passage of the levy, and he was very opposed to its passage.

Now here we have two highly intelligent (our IQs have consistently been measured in triple digits) guys who could not readily reach consensus about whether a four- or five-word sign was pretty. How could we ever hope to settle on the mega-more-complicated issue it represents?

Yet many people seem to have found a path to either totally support the levy or are dead set against it. And they only need a dozen or fewer words to express why - "throwing money at schools doesn't make them better" or "don't our kids deserve the best?" Others are undecided and yearn for clarity. Lots o' luck.

Let's meditate on it for a bit.

Everybody thinks the schools are theirs.

What school is

Teachers see schools as their place to earn a living, practice their craft and sculpt their identities. They see young people parade through, give off some sparks and then move on. Not too bad a life if only "the administration" wouldn't mandate "all those rules."

For students it's a social club with dues that require them to feign interest in sonnets, triangles and legislative branches.

> **"I am in waaaay over my head."**

Parents think of it as a crib for their youngsters and a place for molding and pacifying them.

Taxpayers? Schools are their property because they buy and pay for them, though there is something bogus about this ownership. Like when one owns a few shares of Coca Cola but still has to put quarters in vending machines when thirsty.

Administrators see schools as places to earn a living, practice their craft and sculpt their identities. Not too bad a life except the students and teachers always strain at the few simple rules set out for them for their own good.

I oversimplified, generalized and got a little smart-alecky in that last section, didn't I?

Nevertheless, there are differing points of view on how to make schools excellent. It is, you cannot deny, complicated. You and I must not vote on the levy having synthesized the whole question down to a single thought expressible as a simple phrase.

To cast an informed levy vote we should know how schools are funded and how levy money will be put to use.

But geez, Louise. Every explanation I have ever read or heard — for or against — has been either too glib or incomprehensible. In other words, I'm stumped.

District 742

Now let's get more specific about our "Land of 742." Is ours one of the nation's most chaotic and mis-

> **❝I oversimplified, generalized and got a little smart-alecky. ❞**

managed school districts? How would we know? I've heard the buzz. But maybe the buzz is wrong. Or hardly true at all except that the district's information management is deeply flawed.

I've hired some of the district's output when they were pretty sharp, hard-working young people who are now pretty successful grown-ups. How can that be?

So, is throwing money (that is, passing the levy) at our district a good idea? Well, if the district is mismanaged into chaos and dysfunction, more money will only make it more chaotic and dysfunctional.

On the other hand, if these schools already are doing quite a good job and are strapped for money, providing additional resources (that is, passing the levy) will accrue to the progress of our young people and our communities. It will be a terrific investment.

Should we pass the levy or not? I don't know. I will continue to attempt to reach an informed opinion even while I am pessimistic of my success. Nevertheless, I think I know already how I'm going to vote. I'm going to vote for the levy.

I'm going to vote for the levy because in the absence of solid evidence to the contrary, I am going to choose to have some faith in those who take on these tough, complicated jobs. Teachers, yes. Administrators, yes. And me, who also is voting for new school board members. Yes, I am going to trust me — and you.

And because when I was a student, my parents — and yours — had some faith. And invested. In us. How can I not do the same?

To vote against the levy, I would need certainty.

To vote for it, all I need is a little faith.

Originally published on 10.24.2003
Copyright *St. Cloud Times*

Good players won the games, but they kept coming back to a great coach

"I think I had better go up and get started on a column. I'm getting panicky, I'm stumped for a topic."

"Why don't you write about what you saw at yesterday's game."

"What's to say that hasn't already been said? Should I say that it was cold and clear, a great fall day for football? These details have been recorded and archived at the weather bureau."

"You said it was a very, very good game; that you'd never seen one in which the lead changed hands so many times. You said the plays were frequently spectacular and bizarre."

"Yes, but all the game's details have been amply and elegantly written about and distributed, so no one needs me to describe the action."

"Maybe if you wrote about it from an oblique angle. Write up the game as if you were a food critic. Describe the subtle variations in the half-dozen hot dogs you ate. Or report on the game from the perspective of an innocent -- a primitive, noble savage or a visitor from another culture or planet: 'The gathering was large. The raiment of the cherished tribal representatives was crimson, that of the challengers, gold. All had strange numerical markings on their backs'."

"Nah."

"Well, go give something a try, you're starting to mope."

"I suppose you're right."

It was fall football at its Minnesota best, with winter again not far away. Such a day portends that soon — no matter what — all will be silent and much will be no more. (Internal editor: A bit maudlin, but it's a start.)

It was more than a game. It was a championship game. But it was more than that; a national record, nationally noted, was soon to fall, and most in the throng wanted it to tumble today. Not next week. Today. The presence of a worthy foe and big-time media sports organizations and mostly us had come into alignment. We will have a victory!

And we got it.

Afterward, so much of the reporting was about how humble the coach was about "the record" and how amazed we should be that he can be so humble.

Well, I'm not sure that we ought to be so surprised because we can guess how the coach, St. John's University's John Gagliardi, looks upon it.

> **"Humanly good, not just footbally good."**

Perhaps he is unconvinced "the record" is so great. After all, mostly what he did, he might think, was not get tired of his job. All he had to do was fight the occasional urge to "do something else" — say — sell insurance. He didn't do anything; time's steady, relentless passing did most of it.

He probably also is aware that such a record requires a person maintain good health, which is somewhat out of one's control.

Yes, all one has to do to become a national hero is to do it quite well and keep on doing it. Keep on keeping on. Admirable, but great?

Well, John and sports fans, longevity alone will not do. In the aggregate, coaches win half their games. This "409" accomplishment requires winning most of one's games. No human being has lived long enough to have piled up the necessary sum to set this record without winning most. Had Gagliardi merely won an amazing 60 percent of his games, he would now be at about win number 315, not 409.

So he has been doing a very good job a very long time. His answer for that is that he doesn't win the games. His players do. He says this often and I believe these are not empty words. He means it.

> **"Describe the subtle variations in the half-dozen hot dogs you ate."**

Here's what I think is a measure of his real success: So many of his players — most I think — come back to see him on a regular basis. To see him, to touch base, to be in the same room. He mattered and matters to them. He must have done something good for a long time, too. Humanly good, not just footbally good.

Here's another reason John Gagliardi does not marvel at his accumulation of triumphs. Remember, I am just guessing without authorization and at a certain distance. He started his coaching when football was not a big deal. When he started the now-adored NFL was largely unknown. Gagliardi was born and raised in the briar patch of football as a schoolboy game. No more important than that, even though everyone seems to be treating it as if it is.

He also knows it is this attributed importance that has brought him fame. He sees other people show up at their jobs, enable for their families, volunteer charitably at multiple organizations with great quality and great dependability for many years. And do so without thought of recognition. And when and if accolades come to them — at lesser, more private ceremonies — these diligent citizens, too, are amazed at the fuss.

That's what I thought I saw at the game. But you were there; you saw it.

Originally published on 11.24.2003
Copyright *St. Cloud Times*

Well, wasn't it a lovely Christmas?

The parties, the family, the food, the traveling, the drinking and making merry, the decorations of red and green, the gift buying, the gift giving, the gift getting, the gift wrapping, the gift unwrapping, the gift returning.

Let's see, have we left anything out?

No, I don't believe we have. Still, I keep thinking we may have forgotten something important.

I'll go back to the first paragraph and see what's missing. Go get a Russian tea cake while I put you on hold.

I'm back, and I am quite certain we didn't forget a thing about Christmas.

So, now it is time to straighten up and think about the future because there it is right in front of us: 2004! Yikes.

So what comes to mind as I stare at all the gift residue and detritus? Try this: (on next page)

Originally published on 12.26.2003
Copyright *St. Cloud Times*

> **"Go get a Russian tea cake while I put you on hold"**

We
sure
buy a
lot of stuff.
Which means we
have to
make enough money.
To buy even more stuff. Which
means we need two wage earners. Which
means we have
to buy more stuff. Which means
we don't have enough money. Which
means we have to save money. Which means
we have to buy stuff cheaper. Which means the store
must lower its prices.
Which means workers must get
paid less. Which means they can't
buy as much and some smaller stores close.
Which means the economy is hurt. Which means
we create a stimulus package. To buy stuff. Cheaper.
From "off-shore" manufacturers. Which means we lose more jobs.
Because they pay workers even
less. Especially children. Which is oppressive.
Which means de-stabilized governments. Which means
we feel nervous. Which means we prop 'em up. Which means we can
keep
keep on buying
stuff. Which means
the whole rigama-
role goes on and
on. Forever? Which
means that maybe

we did forget something.

Some anti-abortion activists often back policies that could lead to death

People who profess to care about life? You know, anti-abortion?
We Centriminnians are unsurpassed. Hey, we're No. 1!

So much so that to abort anyone's political career in Central Minnesota, all you have to do is have it waft and drift that the candidate is a bit squishy-soft on abortion. That he/she is not concerned enough about human life.

In which case, that career is over. We elect only people who are sufficiently, that is deeply, "concerned."

Yet, we and the officials we elect — and I want you to picture me pounding my fists on a table while turning a little purple — ain't concerned enough! Not for this buckaroo, your columnist. No sirreee.

I accuse as follows: Our anti-abortion movement professes deeply (fists still pounding) but its focus is too narrow. Waaay too narrow for the true-blue sensitivities of my bleeding heart. Narrow? Heck, it's singular. And there's the rub.

Have you heard the metaphor of a river a mile wide but only a foot deep? How about a river a mile deep but only a foot wide?

Yes, even though we hereabouts can be proud of our intensity, persistence, commitment and durability, it's all and only about that one issue, which comes into play during those months in a life that immediately follow the moment of bliss when Miss Egg meets Mr. Sperm.

OK. On rare occasions we get whipped up for a headline-grabbing event regarding those months at the other end of life — when some unfortunate people are reduced to screaming in agony and wishing in vain to be allowed some help in crafting their own earthly departure. But these people, I'm sure you understand, are soon to be nonvoters, so lots o' luck to them getting their way.

Meritorious as our pro-zygote commitment might be, I wish to offer a few others.

> **❝I want you to picture me pounding my fists on a table while turning a little purple ❞**

Drinking, driving

Let us begin with drinking and driving. Does anyone doubt that — in general — the more you drink, the more likely you are to be involved in a car accident that results in death for innocent people. Thus, is this not a life issue? And is not the concerned-about-life-movement built on the absolute that no consideration trumps the sanctity of life?

Has our concerned-about-human-life movement chimed in on this issue? Nary a peep have I heard.

But what has been the position of all — that's right, all — of this area's law makers about lowering the drunken driving blood-alcohol level to 0.08? They have opposed it. Why? They have offered various reasons ("It will distract the police from chronic drunk drivers." Will it?) Now, however, they are going to pass it. Why? Because it will save lives?

LIFE IS RELATIVE FOR ANTI-ABORTIONISTS

Especially those of moms, dads and other taxpaying voters?

No, because it will allow us to not lose federal highway funds! It is about money, not the hallowed preciousness of life.

Here's another one. In 1997 all your area legislators in office at the time successfully voted to increase Minnesota's speed limits. When it happened, I thought, "People are going to die." A brilliant thought? No, an obvious one.

Did our area's profoundly protective-of-human-life legislators oppose it knowing people would die? Not a one. Did "the movement" raise a fuss? Did they hold feet to the electoral fire? Nary again a peep.

So what has happened since the passage? Big surprise — record state highway deaths have occurred. Dead humans. That is, no longer living. Get it? I don't.

Are we truly "concerned" only when the life has yet to draw its first breath?

> **"Your vote to smote might be frustrated"**

Death penalty

And now, just after the recent holiday time of peace, good will and love, we are turning some serious thoughts toward killing some people. Yes, our Gov. Tim Pawlenty has lent his leadership to making Minnesota a death penalty state.

Closer to home, my queries indicate Sen. Michelle Fischbach and Rep. Bud Heidgerken may go along with it, and Rep. Jim Knoblach and Sen. Dave Kleis are for it. Sen. Betsy Wergin and Rep. Joe Opatz, consistent with professing a status of concern for human life, are against it.

Rep. Dan Severson is the only area legislator who wouldn't answer my inquires. Perhaps he is too busy fighting to restrict your freedom to buy flags unless made in the United States — or other equally urgent matters. (See the Feb. 23 Times for details.)

Minnesota — a death penalty state. Won't we be proud! How enlightened! How progressive! How thoughtful! How modern!

But it is not a sure thing, folks, your vote to smote may be frustrated by some lily livers who oppose it. So, what we need to do is join our children each night as we update and say our prayers:

"Now I lay me down to sleep,

I pray the Lord my soul to keep.

Should a heinous crime make us irate

Grant Minnesota to be a death-penalty state.

God bless Mommy and Daddy ... "

Originally published on 01.23.2004
Copyright St. Cloud Times

Americans lose out on jobs because labor is cheaper elsewhere

A Jan. 17 Times article wondered if Electrolux would be closing its St. Cloud plant (1,800 jobs) next. There was a phrase in the article — headlined "Mayor talks Electrolux's future" — that almost slipped by me: "... where labor is less costly."

Not very alarming, is it? But I smelled a euphemism.

The entire sentence was, "Electrolux expects to save $81 million a year by moving Greenville (its Michigan plant) work to Mexico, where labor is less costly." You're still not freaking out, are you? That's the problem.

Euphemisms are crafted to soothe and be a bit deceptive, and sometimes that's OK. Uncle Howard's "passing away" is an appropriately gentler way of informing Aunt Tillie that "Uncle Howard dropped dead; yup, deader than a door nail."

But let me rewrite the end of that Electrolux sentence more bluntly, " ... moving Greenville work to Mexico, where the company can get away with paying workers less money."

> **❝I smell a euphemism. ❞**

Why can they pay less in Mexico? Is it because Mexicans don't have a choice or know any better? Is it because Mexicans are not quite as productive as Americans? Or are they more productive? Is it because they're — come on, don't make me say it — not like us? You know, sub-American?

MARK THELEN

Many will say the answer is "that is just how the global free-market system works." Or "migration to efficient sources of labor is in the long-term interests of everyone." Or "have an obligation to one's stock holders to maximize return on invested capital."

These are tenets and, once accepted, require no further explanation and no further thought. They express how things are. And that, amigo, is that.

The Times' offending phrase was almost not noteworthy in the context of our national tolerance of what is happening to labor and jobs in America. We are steadily losing productive jobs. First farm, then manufacturing, now technical and professional jobs. If we continue to do so, this country is on its way to its knees.

And — sorry to be such a killjoy — even when you hear something along the lines of "100,000 jobs were created last month," be sure to wonder if it was the result of 400,000 new jobs being gained offering "fewer hours at lesser wages and lower benefits" while 300,000 higher-paying jobs were lost.

See the Times' Feb. 15 piece "More workers struggle with lower paying jobs."

This just in!

I just heard this on the radio: The State of Minnesota has awarded its Human Resources Hot Line contract; the phones will now be answered from India.

This just in, too!

> "Job openings for laundry and dry cleaning workers in
> Minnesota are expected to rise 11.2 percent, from 4,052 to
> 4,506 between 2000 and 2010."

> — Jan. 25 Star Tribune

Maybe that phrase "where labor is less costly" was so vivid to me
because I was still masticating on President Bush's recent comment
and the fact that I had heard no one shriek in objection.

Our president said, "If an American employer is offering a job that
American citizens are not willing to take, we ought to welcome into
our country a person who will fill that job."

Didn't it strike anyone that what would follow could have been,
(shudder) " ... and if they aren't willing to take it, perhaps we'll need
to find a few mules that will"?

I must be a little off base here because there was not only no national
outcry, there was nary a whimper or a peep. It gets lonely.

Why won't Americans take these jobs? They would if these jobs paid
more. Why don't they pay more? Because there are — and we could
sure use a euphemism here — "alien" workers desperate enough to
take them.

If there weren't such workers, the wages for these unpleasant jobs would
go up and some American workers would take them. The TV show
"Fear Factor" demonstrates that even handsome, healthy Americans
will eat heaps of disgusting larvae and bed down with scorpions if the
cash is right.

American workers must fight it out for American jobs because we:

- Import non-American workers to American jobs — the Bush phenomenon above.

- Export American jobs to non-American workers — the Electrolux phenomenon.

Isolation? Tariffs? Closed borders? Fortress America? Wage supports? Tear down NAFTA? Withdraw from the World Trade Organization? Trust the free-market system? Pray that God will bless America?

Sorry, no solutions, but let's try an explanation.

> **"Even handsome, healthy Americans will eat heaps of disgusting larvae and bed down with scorpions."**

Political opportunists are more concerned with delivering goodies to their political base of wealthy corporation executives — the only people who benefit from labor surpluses — regardless of long-term consequences.

Profits and getting elected are being placed above the nation and its people.

Originally published on 02.27.2004

Copyright St. Cloud Times

Get out the tax tables, then figure out who's not twisting the numbers

Tax cuts for whom?

Somebody's lyin'. Oh, all right maybe that's a bit strong. Maybe.

One side says — I am morphing all of what they say on the subject into a single phrase — "Tax cuts for the rich."

The other side says — more morphing — "Economic stimulus tax cuts for all Americans."

And every time I hear either side speak, I wonder why someone doesn't get out the tax tables and do a little calculatin'. We all have to do it. We're doing it now — it's tax time!

How hard can it be to settle this thing?

It's just arithmetic. Let's get out the tax tables for 2002 and those projected for 2004; let's see what the tax savings would be for a married couple at various income levels and — voila — we know who's telling the truth.

Feeling a wave of responsibility I asked my tax accountant, Karen, "What do you think?"

She said something along the lines that it might be a little more complicated.

I interpreted that to mean that my idea had considerable merit.

Besides, what could it be more simplistic than " ... for the rich" or " ... for all Americans"? Heartened by the utterly unadorned utterances of our leaders, I plunged.

Charts and table are nice. They lend an authoritativeness to research.

The table below shows the relative size of the cuts as a percentage of taxable income.

The two-column chart shows the growth of the tax cuts as income rises.

It is clear from these charts that (except for taxable incomes less than $10,000) there are indeed "tax cuts for all Americans."

It is also clear that these are dang fine "tax cuts for the rich."

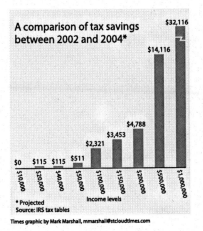

A comparison of tax savings between 2002 and 2004*

$32,116
$14,116
$4,788
$3,453
$2,321
$0 $115 $115 $511

Income levels
* Projected
Source: IRS tax tables

Times graphic by Mark Marshall, mmarshall@stcloudtimes.com

So, both sides are technically telling the truth. And they will, no doubt, continue to do so.

From my analysis, though, one side is telling the honest truth and the other side is shading it. It is up to you to decide whose side I'm on.

Better yet, whose side are you on?

As you do your taxes and realize your savings, count your blessings.

Originally published on 03.26.2004
Copyright St. Cloud Times

Get government out of marriage process, let religions offer choices

"We'll go extinct," warned Sartell/Sauk Rapids-area Rep. Dan Severson in the March 24 Times.

President Bush finds it "troubling." His first lady tells us many find it "shocking" and the nation is experiencing "jolts."

The issue is gay marriage.

But dread not, I can solve and salve simply by activating conservative principles that transcend the issue and give clarity. Get out a pen, you'll want to do some underlining.

Our Constitution identifies as an inalienable right, "the pursuit of happiness." An excellent way for two people to pursue happiness is to make a lifetime commitment of love and fidelity. That should settle it.

It doesn't?

Two other boulders of bedrock conservatism are government not intruding in the private affairs of, and not imposing religious beliefs upon, its citizens.

The application of these two to marriage is self-evident. So there.

Tough choices

Many of my co-conservatives, however, seem to feel so deeply about gay marriages that they are turning their backs on such principles.

Feelings or principles? Choose. Yes, it is tough, but that is why we have principles.

Those wishing to enter same-gender marriages offer identical reasons to those of us who have "chosen" mixed gender marriages. Examples are

"He/she is noble, kind and good and I want to spend my life with him/her, her/her or him/him" and "He/she has a hot bod and is really good in the sack."

Speaking of "good in the sack," more of Severson's wisdom has application here. He points out that "marriage isn't about lust (n. strong sexual desire) ... "

Ouch, I'm sure those of us who have experienced tingling within our marriages will want to immediately make some changes. Cold shower, anyone?

Reasons given in opposition to gay marriage are that such unions are forbidden by their (but not everyone's) religious beliefs. Or that "marriage is only for having children" — which would exclude our Aunt Tillie — 86 and now 43 years without a uterus — from her sixth and last shot at true happiness; that being Renaldo, 91, up at Mother of Mercy in Albany.

Or that it would be destructive to "the institution of marriage." To which I ask, "Will it cause harm to your marriage?" Not mine.

> **"Aunt Tillie – 86 and now 43 years without a uterus "**

Will anyone ever say, "Muffin, have you noticed the zip and commitment has gone out of our marriage since gays started getting hitched?"

To which she responds, "Hey, couples are breaking up throughout the subdivision."

Feelings

> "I don't like it, let's make it illegal."
>
> — Lionel, national talk show host, March 31

My guess is that most people's opposition to gay marriages is "feelings" — the thought of it makes them *feel* ill. Such feelings should not be the stuff of legislation, much less the Constitution.

So they fabricate reasons, principally from the Bible. But I'll be darned if I can find a word about it in "The Two Great Commandments" or the Sermon on the Mount or any of the other big ideas that came from Jesus. If you can find a reference, I'll bet it is within a verse or two of the one about us bald guys being unclean.

But, hey, I don't wish to change people's minds, I just wish to show both sides a graceful way out of the fracas. I am a uniter, not a divider.

Here's what we do: Get government out — O-U-T — out of the marriage business all together. It will remain only in the civil-union business, bestowing and assuring civil rights.

> **"Muffin, have you noticed the zip and commitment has gone out of our marriage?"**

Marriages will be performed by religions — always granting civil rights but also whatever restrictions, conditions, rules and blessings they care to include. Some will offer gay marriages; some will freak out at the thought. Shop around.

But let us expand our thinking and not restrict this marrying to religions.

Let us open it to other groups to which people feel strong affinity. Like Rotary Club. Or the U.S. Marine Corps: Semper Fidelis "Always Faithful." Very romantic.

How about a Green Bay Packers wedding? Green tuxes for the men, golden gowns for the ladies. Oops, there I go thinking man and woman again. Ducks Unlimited. AARP. NASCAR!

Certainly you will be able to find a marriage provider group that will have just the "features" you want. You go there, get married, then for the rest of your life, proudly proclaim "Ours is a Lutheran-Missouri Synod marriage." or "Ours is a Future Farmers of America marriage."

"Johnny-Benny" marriages are already common, so let's give the lovers trademark status.

And why should private enterprise's profit motive be locked out? A Marshall Fields wedding for some, Wal-Mart for others. How about a Mercedes-Benz wedding? A Bank of America wedding? A Tiffany wedding has a ring to it. Get it? Tiffany Wedding Ring.

You can tell, can't you, it is all going to be loads of fun. Unless you don't want to have fun. In which case, maybe you shouldn't be thinking about marriage.

It's a matter of principle.

Originally published on 04.23.2004
Copyright St. Cloud Times

Representative's real constituency is Republican leadership

About a month ago, the Times reported that Minnesota Rep. Jim Knoblach would not support a bill to extend the area sales taxes despite having been asked to do so by many local officials.

The sales tax, as painlessly as possible, funds vital community necessities and niceties: an invigorated regional library, road improvements and keeping our tetraplex competitive with improvements to the St. Cloud Civic Center. It was reported that he was "uncomfortable with it."

Three days later, whammo, the Times reported the Ways and Means Committee "chops Northstar (commuter line) from bonding bill." And who is the powerful chair of the powerful Ways and Means Committee? How did you ever guess?

But perhaps it was to save taxpayer dollars. Nooooooo.

The report said "The amendment ... divides the money ... among a variety of projects ... and most of the projects are in the districts of the Ways and Means Committee members." But our chair's district got none of the $37.5 million.

This time, Knoblach commented that it "sets a bad precedent."

Sets a bad precedent? For many, his failure is an outrage.

Knoblach knows of the many people from the many local organizations who have worked the many hours — as volunteers (and without per diem) — to make this happen. He should have gotten it done.

The amendment was not the result of partisan bickering. It was proposed

by a Republican
and passed by an
18-10 vote.
The Star Tribune
on the same day

"Knobloch mystifies me."

reported the bill "pitted so many members of the GOP majority against
the governor (Tim Pawlenty), speaker (Steve Sviggum) and committee
chairman (our guy) — all Republicans and all Northstar supporters —
that one DFL legislator said she was witnessing 'a palace coup.'"

Knoblach mystifies me. Our streets should be paved with gold. Good
things should be coming our way. This should be Central Minnesota's
golden era.

We have the chairman of the House Ways and Means Committee as
one of our legislators. In a Republican controlled House with a
Republican Governor.

What do we get? See "bad precedent" and "uncomfortable" above;
we get Hamlet.

Nothing new

These roadblocks are nothing new. I first noticed them in 1999 when I
had the opportunity to work with dozens of organizations and hundreds
of individuals to try to pass a Community Assets Referendum.

This would have created local sales taxes to fund parks and trails,
improvements to Whitney Senior Center, other community centers,
libraries, soccer and softball fields and a regionally significant events
center that would have provided activities and fun for everyone,

including providing a home for St. Cloud State University football.

And the state would have given us as much as $25 million.

Well, we have the sales tax anyhow — if you even noticed? And SCSU has had to build a separate facility to play its four or five home football games at a cost of millions to taxpayers.

So we end up with all of the downside to the Community Assets Referendum and few of the community assets.

No fewer than 20 times leading up to that community referendum vote were there extraneous, often anguished items prominently featured in this newspaper by or about Knoblach.

A few examples: "Events Center ballot won't split," April 20. "Knoblach can't fight for more events center funds," Aug. 9, and "Knoblach chills center's chances," Aug. 10.

Had it not been for his intrusion into the process, surely a mere 181 votes of the 13,898 cast would have been cast differently and Central Minnesota would be better off today.

The Times editorial board, three weeks before that election, took this position: "Knoblach has gone to great lengths to say he is neutral on

"With legislative representation like this, who needs legislative roadblocks?"

the issue ... we have to wonder if he ever was ... (He has struck) a big blow to backers of the plan ... he did not honor his vow to stay neutral on the issue. The question is ... about his honesty with constituents."

Roadblocks

With legislative representation like this, who needs legislative roadblocks?

Why doesn't he represent his district and his constituents? I have some ideas and wish to offer a scenario:

• He doesn't need to raise money for his re-election, money is not an issue for him. Besides, he will win re-election because no area House seat has seen an incumbent voted out of office in this entire area in more than 30 years!

• His real constituency is the Republican leadership. He sees a bright future for himself and he's not deluded so long as he curries their favor. They are, largely, suburban Twin Cities people. They hate sales taxes because they don't need them. They hate Northstar because they don't have to get to the metro area; they are already there.

• Keep playing his house leadership cards right and he can run for Mark Kennedy's seat for the U.S. House in 2006 when Kennedy decides to go for Mark Dayton's U.S. Senate seat.

Or something like that. Hang on to this column, in two years we'll know.

Originally published on 05.28.2004

Downtown is full of fun, free places to explore

Perhaps I have been a little grim lately.

Just last month I was compelled to scold the cherubic smile right off the face of an area legislator. Before that it was necessary to settle a tax issue and alert you to the gloom of jobs going offshore. Although we did have some fun with pro-life issues and same-gender marriages, didn't we?

So, this month, how about something wholesome and cheerful, seasoned with boosterism and thrift?

> **"Look at all those balls. "**

I enlisted the help of the very wholesome Lori and Brian Barrick family — he's a senior designer at Thelen Advertising — including their three children, Tate, Tara and Kale, age 5, 3 and 3 months.

I enlisted the Barricks to test ride the new, old, free Downtown Trolley.

"We get to take that!?!"
— Tara.

They were to hop on and off a number of times along its figure-eight route and take in some of the really neat free stuff in their and your downtown St. Cloud.

The idea is to get you to do it, too. And to do so, I have made some suggestions and sprinkled some comments from the Barrick expedition.

Adventuring

Let's say your first trolley exit is the Civic Center. Take the main
entrance and walk all the way to the back where you step outside onto
a balcony and gasp as you enjoy an elevated panorama of one of the
world's great rivers, the Mississippi. On your way out, peek at the
Baseball Hall of Fame.

> "Look at all those balls."
> —Tate.

Back outside the Civic Center entrance, look straight ahead: The
Radisson. Stroll through its lobby, real casual, like you're a guest, and
take the elevator to the eighth floor. It's one of those glass ones on the
outside of the building. This time you'll be gazing and gasping westerly.

> "It's scary."
> —Tara, quickly taking a position on the elevator floor.

So as to not completely rip off the Rad, some of you make a reservation
in its Chanticleer Room, one of only two Central Minnesota restaurants
that can truly be called fine dining. (The other is Cork's, not on
today's route.)

Now leave the Radisson and cross the street to the upstairs/south in the
Red Carpet. You will find thousands of square feet of elegant, newly and
brilliantly refurbished Martini Lounge. Oh, yes — notice all the ceiling
and wall fans powered by one motor; trust me, it's unique. Here you can
gawk for free or have a refreshment — remember, you're not driving,
you're trolleying. Or vow to return one night to show the place off to
out-of-towners. They'll wish they were more like you and lived here too.
The desired effect.

Real downtown

Get back on the trolley. Get off at the true heart of downtown, Seventh and St. Germain. See there, right next to Quizno's? The global headquarters of Thelen Advertising. But don't go in, they're busy and there's not much to be had that's free in there. Instead, go into the Centre Square atrium between Ciatti's and Herberger's.
Look up; nice, huh?

> "Ooooooo."
> — Kale.

Back on the trolley. Down St. Germain to whatever they call Zapp Bank these days. Exit. Walk in, only about 20 feet. Look. Nice. Now across the street to whatever they call the classy, glassy Security Federal Building these days. Another great elevator ride, looking through a gigantic wall of glass toward the southeast. See the grassy knoll/underpass where Kennedy got shot? Of course you don't, but this view is similar in layout and scale.

Back on the trolley. Still free. Heading west until it is ready to turn right. Look, see Mark Suess' Found Objects? Go in. It's like a museum and there's

"Midday funerals can be fun."

only one of these stores in the whole world. He ought to charge admission. When I was there, he had a humongous dining room set with a cosmic price tag and a armoire for almost as much. But worth it!
But also a lot of stuff for $10 and $39 from all over the world. All interesting. They ought to charge admission. Oh, I said that already?

Back on the trolley. To the courthouse. Have your kids seen the inside of it yet? They haven't?

"It's so big!"
— Tara.

"It makes a lot of noise."
— Tate.

"He means it makes an echo."
— Daddy.

Don't be afraid to go upstairs to one of the big courtrooms — fabulous decor and most of the time empty. If a trial is going on, so much the better, maybe someone gets sent to the big house.

Gosh my gushes, I am running out of room. But I wanted to tell you about the talking elevator in the Daniel Building, 11 Seventh Ave. N. And the Paramount Theatre. And the Cathedral — midday funerals can be fun. These are often open to free peeks.

And I haven't even told you the trolley's route includes the Gardens Munsinger and Clemens ... and ... and ...

"I work downtown every day. It's about time I took the opportunity to look at it more closely. "
— Brian.

"Downtown is really something. It's so easy to forget it has all this."
— Lori.

"Mommy, can we ride the trolley again?"
— Tara.

Originally published on 06.25.2004

Copyright St. Cloud Times

Organization should be consensus builder, stay away from partisanship

"Whatever you do, don't talk about religion or politics."

Good advice

Strolling downtown in nearby Buffalo, I noticed a storefront indicating it housed their local Chamber of Commerce. An intuitive flash (not quite a thought) was that it was a friendly shop where I could obtain a free map, learn the name of a reliable real estate agent or get a list of commercial properties suitable for locating a new factory or a book store.

I felt that this was not a place where broad political issues were hashed, nor who is the better of two local "favorites" because one is more this way on light rail, or welfare or education or taxes.

The St. Cloud Area Chamber of Commerce — unencumbered by a lack of enthusiastic leadership on the part of its Executive Director Teresa Bohnen — does get involved in such discussions and activities. I think it is unwise.

It has created a Political Action Committee and it has an active political affairs committee. The PAC is separate from the Chamber, but its actions will always be seen as those of the Chamber.

The political affairs committee — a forum for discussion of political issues and the people involved — is a very good idea. But ours has become quite partisan and stages events that are decidedly anti-tax, anti-government and pro-Republican.

What sparked this column at this time? Page 19 of the current issue of the local Chamber's publication, Business Central. It is a full page of pictures and accompanying captions. Eight images of Republican office holders huddling and smiling with Chamber folks. No independents, nonaffiliateds and no Democrats.

That proves nothing, but it sure fit comfortably into my bulging apperceptive file filled with similar stuff. It keeps adding up.

Similar views

And I am not alone in my opinion. In preparation for this column, I had discussions. One member recovered a green Chamber mailing from his wastebasket about the 2004 legislative session. He said to me, "What's this all about?" reading a paragraph "gratuitously" praising the efforts of a single area Republican.

Another local eminence retrieved the agenda of the Chamber-organized "2004 Transportation Forum." He had circled the speakers' names. He said, "Look, four Republicans, David Olson of the Minnesota Chamber and Teresa Bohnen." A slanted and typical slate, we agreed. Are you miffed I'm writing this? If so, is it because I am wrong? Or is it because you cherish the bias and wish it to continue without comment?

Yes, the Chamber has — in effect — leaned heavily to one side. And admittedly, its leanings are not mine.

My leanings are that it wasn't independent business that made our nation great; it was the balance between government and business that did. America did not invent a lust for self-fulfillment. It invented a government that allowed and limited our freedom to make a buck. Quite a moderate leaning, don't you think?

Problems

Anti-tax and anti-government is now a popular chant and our Chamber has gleefully picked up the tune.

Here's the problem: It now — regularly and in so many forms — deals with issues likely to get some members all whipped up. And angry. And threaten to withhold membership dues. And some of these dues are larger than others. Much larger. Much much. And money talks.

In the last go-round, when the PAC — I was a member — did not endorse an incumbent local Republican Senate candidate, all hell broke loose. Subsequently, a PAC member's career was compromised when his "confidential" vote was leaked to the vexed candidate. Irritated and interested Chamber members made late night vituperative phone calls. The PAC's response was feckless and timid.

Who needs that? I could be next, so I was out of there.

Unlike other Chambers, ours encourages nonbusiness membership such as from educational institutions. So far, these members have been pretty good sports about the Chamber's new anti-tax climate. And remember, to education, anti-tax is anti-funding and anti-revenue. How much longer will your schools pay for Chamber membership dues, knowing that it is biting the hand that feeds them?

Our Chamber, in lock step with the Minnesota Chamber, opposed Local Government Aid. LGA is a program to reduce local property taxes. (By the way, the Chamber

"Go figure — but do it in Wonderland"

sends out a yearly invoice to the city of St. Cloud for almost $2,000 for its annual membership.)

In effect, your tax-supported Chamber worked so the state would reduce funding to your local government so that your property taxes rise.

Your tax dollars working to increase your tax dollars. Go figure — but do it in Wonderland.

Additionally, not all business people think alike. A partisan Chamber will please only some of its members all the time. A nonpartisan but politically active Chamber will please most members hardly ever. Such is the basis of the wisdom at the top of this column.

Our local Chamber should be neither. It should go back to being a consensus builder and a booster of the total community and its commerce. That's why members join in the first place.

Originally published on 07.23.2004
Copyright St. Cloud Times

Potential office holders shouldn't feel nervous about quick quiz on facts

Basal intelligence is necessary — but not sufficient — for elected officials to properly represent their citizens. Such brain power is not necessary, however, in order for them to get elected.

What I have in mind is a bit of mischief — it is true my name is an anagram for "rankle them" — mixed in with good citizenship.

What I have in mind is attending (you and me; in separate cars) just about every forum (the summer's over, here they come) at which concerned voters will be allowed to question those running for office.

Or just wait for them to come knocking on your door.

> **"My name is an anagram for "rankle them." "**

I don't want us to ask the usual questions such as "Do you support family values?" "Do you favor quality education for our children?" "Do you believe that if monsters are coming to eat us that we ought to adequately fund our nation's defense?"

All candidates have been instructed how to respond to — not necessarily answer — such inquiries. What I want to know is:

• Mr./Ms. Candidate for public office, without using a pencil or a calculator, how much is 9 times 13?

• Who was president of the United States during the American Civil War?

• Please define and spell appropriation.

You see, candidates for positions as leaders and policy makers should find questions such as these laughably easy. But some of them won't, and I think they ought to be discovered before Election Day.

I have had enough encounters with elected officials to know that some of them have IQs that could be considered a comfortable room temperature.

I'd say about a third of them. No, that's not fair; about 20 percent.

Hey, there's a good one — ask the next officeholder you meet to tell you what the difference is between "a third" and "20 percent." Then enjoy as he furrows his vast brow searching an exit to this line of inquiry.

Fence posts, especially old ones, say nothing and thus appear wise in comparison to some recent office holders. No names here, but if you happen to see me on the street, let's compare notes.

The St. Cloud Area Chamber of Commerce has an affiliated political action committee. Once — those were sunnier times — I was a member. The PAC hosted a number of candidate forums. I made the suggestion to ask questions such as these. It laid an egg. I think the other members thought it would make the candidates uncomfortable.

Well, duh.

I still think it is a good idea and I know there are zany patriots, my friends, out there already making lists of questions.Coming up with the questions can be fun, a real family affair and a lesson in good government. Remember, I want the questions to be easy enough for the smartest fifth-grader in your neighborhood to answer off the top of her head.

I don't expect them to know the capital of Uzbekistan (Tashkent), but it would be nice if they know the capital of Saudi Arabia (Riyadh.) They really should know the capitals of our neighboring states — presuming they can identify our neighboring states.

And I wouldn't worry too much about asking questions that are too easy; There aren't that many. Here are examples: "Can you spell your name?" "How old are you?" and "Count to five." Too easy even for this purpose.

Here's some more good ones:

• How far from Earth is our moon? Cut them slack, any answer between 50,000 and 1 million miles is good enough; they've got the general idea. 150 miles is wrong.

• Where was Beethoven born? I will be delighted if they answer Austria or Germany. Even Europe. Philadelphia is incorrect.

• How long a time is four score and seven years.

• When it's 10 o'clock in Sartell, what time is it in New York?

If you ask them, "What is the boiling point of water?" and they respond with "Fahrenheit, Centigrade Kelvin or Absolute?" you may excuse her from answering; she passes.

For a big majority, the answers to well-crafted questions should be easy. They will be glad you asked. But to those who are made to feel uncomfortable, well, who wants them on any city council or in St. Paul telling you how to live?

The idea here is not to embarrass the candidates you do not like and glorify your favorites. This should be fair and nonpartisan, so shuffle your questions. I want this

> **"Some of them have IQs that could be considered a comfortable room temperature."**

exercise to accomplish only one thing: to distinguish between the adequate and those who should develop a keener sense of their own limitations.

Be polite. Use, do not abuse. If it turns out to be fun for you and a squirming moment for them, well, that's not your fault. People seeking office without a head on their shoulders should be exposed.

Originally published on 08.27.2004
Copyright St. Cloud Times

Board should back renewal of half-cent sales tax to fund library, other projects

Boggling: Your local Chamber of Commerce doesn't seem to be getting behind an initiative to bring about important improvements to our regional airport. Certainly a vigorous modern airport facility is beloved of any region's commerce.

I am referring to the Nov. 2 referendum requesting the Legislature to allow the renewal of our half-cent sales tax to fund a new regional library, an aquatic center (think Becker, only bigger!) and other projects such as all of the above and below.

Stupefying: Our Convention and Visitors Bureau — it is a division of the Chamber — has not joined the same effort to expand our Civic Center, which is its marquee venue for its prime directive, attracting meetings and conventions. All of the CVB's funding is from local sales taxation — but (for now) it answers to the Chamber's board. Conflicted, wouldn't you say?

Befuddling: Improvements to our regionally useful roadways? Our Chamber doesn't seem to be lending a hand.

Why is the Chamber not helping gain passage of this important measure? I am left to speculate: It actually likes all of the projects but wishes, as with moonbeams, they were free.

"As disgusting as flesh eating bacteria"

Yes, the Chamber wants them because these projects all

make for better communities and a better climate for commerce.

But it does require a form of taxation, and that could be something the Chamber seems to regard as evil as Satan, as disgusting as flesh eating bacteria!

Go out to eat and spend $35. Your tax? Rounded up, 18 cents. You've been paying it all along. It's so paltry, you just didn't notice. And it does not apply to medicine, groceries or clothing. It is as painless as a tax can be.

This method of raising the money means we don't have to raise property taxes. And people from the region who use our roads, the library, the airport and the Civic Center, they get to chip in. With property taxes, it would all fall to you if you pay a property tax — residential or commercial — in any of the affected locales.

I would think the Chamber would adore a revenue source spread gingerly through the region — for the benefit of the region — all the while avoiding property tax increases for its members.

The Chamber's lack of leadership on this issue has so many of my circuits misfiring, I've got smoke coming out of my ears.

The executive directors of St Cloud's Downtown Council, the Area Economic Development Partnership and St. Cloud Opportunities immediately joined organizations as diverse as Friends of Library and the Trades and Labor Council and started working — in anticipation of their boards' approvals. Two of them quickly received it; the other meets later today and I'll put up big odds, will get it too. But where, oh where, is the Chamber and its CVB?

CHAMBER LAGS ON SALES TAX CAMPAIGN

Will the Chamber yet endorse it? Way back in July it expressed a lack of enthusiasm for something similar to the City Council and has just now, two months later, sent a survey to its members. The results will not go to the board until October. If Chambers have feet, I think ours are dragging.

No, I don't expect much. Maybe a shadowy endorsement proffered without any plan of activism. Possibly this would do more harm than good because it would give many would-be member-supporters the mistaken sense that something is being done.

This to the Chamber board: Please join us. Keep a good thing going. Get behind this multicommunity effort with a vigorous plan of action for passage. Make this columnist eat crow and admit he is dead wrong. He will. Gladly.

In less than two years, the half-cent sales tax has already provided funding for airport runway improvements (without which, George W. would have had to rent a car), the expansion of 10th Street South, and the interchange providing access to the I-94 Business Park and its economic development.

Would the Chamber like to give them back?

These are in addition to the purchase of land for a new Mississippi River park, expanded trails along the Mississippi and replacement of the aged wading pool at Riverside Park with a modern safe splash pad.

The mayors and city councils of Waite Park, Sauk Rapids, Sartell, St Augusta, St. Cloud and St. Joseph essentially want this referendum passed to ensure that many new benefits can begin.

On Nov. 2, let's all vote "yes" for healthier communities and healthier commerce which, I have always thought, overlap.

Author's note:

I have joined a broad-based committee of community enthusiasts to spread the word and encourage passage of this November's referendum. Subsequently, my firm, Thelen Advertising, was hired to assist in the production of some of its informational and promotional material. All of my personal and professional time is donated.

This column highlights an issue about which our current Chamber of Commerce and I disagree. There are enough other disagreements that I have failed to renew my membership of three decades. The opinions expressed here are mine alone.

Originally published on 09.24.2004
Copyright St. Cloud Times

"George W. would have had to rent a car."

Though changes aren't always forthcoming, the victories are worthwhile

A Times Oct. 3 headline read: "Group protests UND mascot."

What? I thought I had put that unpleasantness to rest with my seventh Times Writers Group column way back in March 2001 when I pointed out, "It is irrelevant whether one intends insult or intends honor, the impact is that it causes distress in others, and that is not polite."

Did I think I'd change the world even a little? Yes. Have I? Apparently not: UND still has the same mascot name, and more locally, our Cathedralites are still the Crusaders despite a pontifical apology.

So why do I bother writing a column?

Because I get to grumble, show off and be a smart-aleck on a monthly basis.

Warmest congratulations to me on this, my 50th column, as well as to the other stalwart charter TWGers; Karen Cyson, Frank Kundrat, Linda Larson, Leland Rueb, Ytmar Santiago and Duane Sheppard.

> **"Grumble, show off and be a smart aleck."**

We have endured to about 40,000 words. Indulge me whilst I gaze backward on my experiences during one through 49.

How did I get such a swell assignment? By begging and bragging, how else?

I told the Times I would write "cogently, wittily, persuasively and sardonically about issues" and "... people will smile and wave as they shout out, 'Hey, Mark, that was some article you wrote. You've really influenced me and made my life so much better. Very droll and valuable to the community.' "

It worked; I got the job. It's fun. Did you notice the final sentence of my seventh paragraph? Where else, other than from a pulpit, could one get away with "whilst I gaze"?

Column No. 31 was another failure, a local radio show I call "Hate Talk With the Ox" is still on the air; prevented from being a larger embarrassment to the community only by the fact its audience is meager. It gathers its sour listeners with self-congratulatory amazement at their own brilliance by how able they are at whomping on the "least of (our) brethren."

But wait, in my 13th column, come to think of it, I complained about this newspaper's reportage of various local people and pointed out what I had considered a pattern in which " ... if all you know about them is what you read in our local paper, you think ill of (them)." I even used "lurid."

Well, it's not like I hadn't warned the Times. In my application I also wrote, "I don't much like your paper and feel you could be better if you were more impartially challenged from time to time."

I have not witnessed such reportage since and fantasize that my column (Yes!) might have triggered just such a positive change. At this writing, I admit to a flip-flop and now like the Times. I hope it is not because I am now — a little — "one of them."

Is it fun being a TWG person? Yes, people approach me and say nice things. It's gratifying and I like it a lot. Not once has anyone said a discouraging word. Thank you.

E-mailers are either complimentary, interesting or helpful, like this from Joan S. " ... your column (No. 24) this week sounded like you had swallowed a thesaurus."

She was right. That single column included the words sodden, licentious, denizen, probity, estimable, rectitude, unseemly and intone. (Groan.)

Another responded to my column (No. 34) on the 1920 Duluth lynchings of three innocent black youths, telling at length of her (then 5-year-old) mother's account: "She was scared out of her wits not understanding why her parents would not let her out of the house ... Remember back then children ... were not given ... information about happenings. ... The town was a mess with rioting, noise and terrible rushes of people going by her house ..."

The Times Web site chat, however, is another matter.

My first column was called drivel, my second "boring, a bit braggy and smuggish." And so it has continued for more than four years without pause with such as "(Thelen is) a complete whack job" and "unstable." To which I respond, "Boring? Really?"

Thanks, Tony, for insights that were the start of many of my columns and much of whatever merit could be found in them. Thanks, Ann, for making sure my pronouns agree; but mostly for saying, when it was needed, "No, please do not even try to get this one published; we want to go on living in this community; don't we? You still have time. Go write about something else."